THE
HOT
SAUCE
COOKBOOK

THE
HOT
SAUCE
COOKBOOK

EBURY
PRESS

CONTENTS

MAIN MEALS

DESSERTS, BAKING & DRINKS

INTRODUCTION

Hot sauces are now increasingly popular as more and more people become interested in eating a more varied diet and exploring different world cuisines. Consequently, new types of hot sauces are emerging all the time and there are literally hundreds available, if you include all the regional and artisanal brands as well as the ubiquitous well-known ones.

Hot chilli-based sauces have always played a starring role in Asian, Mexican, Caribbean and Middle Eastern cooking, but now that our taste buds are developing a hankering for spice, they are featuring more prominently in traditional Western dishes, too, as well as being used as a condiment. In the United States, these sauces have such popularity that there are even hot sauce festivals that attract thousands of aficionados, who gather to taste the latest varieties and discover new brands. Once a fringe ethnic food, hot sauces are now hitting the mainstream and most of us have at least one bottle in our kitchen cupboard.

THE BASIC INGREDIENTS

Hot sauces vary in their flavour, colour, texture and intensity of heat, depending on which chilli peppers are used to make them and how they are combined with other ingredients. However, they all contain three essential elements: chillies, vinegar and salt. Sugar, spices, herbs, garlic, tomatoes, vegetables and thickening agents may be added to this holy trinity. Flavourings and colourings are sometimes exotic, as in the case of rose harissa, which incorporates crushed rose petals and rose water.

AROUND THE WORLD

This book celebrates the diversity of hot sauces, capturing the flavours and cultures of their countries of origin. The recipes feature fiery crimson harissa paste from the Levant and North Africa, Thai sweet chilli and Sriracha sauces, West Indian hot pepper sauces, Jamaican jerk sauce, Portuguese and southern African piri piri sauce, South American aji, Mexican Cholula, jalapeño and smoky chipotle chilli sauces, Indonesian sambal oelek, Chinese Szechuan spicy plum sauce and Japanese wasabi, as well as red and green Tabasco from America.

Sriracha is a good example of a hot sauce that has taken off from its humble beginnings in a Thai seaside village to become a global phenomenon. The spread of street food stalls and markets and food and music festivals, as well as the new breed of food bloggers, have helped hot sauces go viral and develop a cult following. Like many other hot sauces that are now mainstream, the appeal of Sriracha lies in its versatility. It has reached out from being solely a condiment in Thai and Vietnamese restaurants to flavouring cookies, cakes and desserts as well as savoury dishes.

RECIPES

In this book we have recipes for hot sauces that you can make from scratch at home, ranging from tomato chilli jam for enhancing cheese and cold meats to unusual variations on harissa, including rose harissa and a green version flavoured with herbs. You can learn how easy it is to cook your own sweet chilli sauce or even Sriracha, and you'll also find hot and spicy salad dressings, salsas, dipping sauces and marinades.

The delicious recipes feature snacks, desserts and drinks as well as breakfasts and brunches, salads and supper dishes. There are old favourites as well as some exciting and innovative dishes from around the world, including Jamaican jerk chicken and 'stamp and go' fritters, Mexican burritos, harissa chicken shawarma wraps and a Peruvian quinoa brunch with aji.

THE APPEAL OF HOT SAUCE

Hot sauces are more than 'just a food', they reveal how cultures can fuse and connect. Even though countries in different parts of the world have their own interpretations, we can all relate to the basic ingredients of chillies, salt and vinegar. There's something very personal, pleasurable and almost spiritual about these three elements – they can transform our mood as well as our palate. So whether you want to just add heat to a soup or spice up a cake or loaf of bread, our hot sauce recipes will show you how.

HOME-MADE
HOT SAUCES

HOT DIPPING SAUCES

Use these sweet and spicy hot sauces for dipping spring rolls, wontons, dim-sum and appetizers, or drizzle them over crabcakes or rice and noodles. They will stimulate your taste buds and enhance your meal.

THAI DIPPING SAUCE

MAKES: APPROX. 60ML/2FL OZ (¼ CUP)
PREP: 5 MINUTES

2 tbsp water
1 tbsp caster (superfine) sugar
2 tbsp nam pla (Thai fish sauce)
juice of 1 lime
2 fresh red bird's eye chillies, thinly sliced
2 spring onions (scallions), finely sliced

1 Put the water and sugar in a bowl and stir until the sugar dissolves.

2 Stir in the remaining ingredients and then transfer to a serving bowl.

OR YOU CAN TRY THIS...
– Add a little chopped coriander (cilantro).
– Add some diced cucumber or shredded carrot.
– Add ½ stalk lemongrass, outer peel removed and finely diced.

VIETNAMESE NUOC CHAM

MAKES: APPROX. 150ML/5FL OZ (⅔ CUP)
PREP: 10 MINUTES | **COOK:** 5 MINUTES

4 tbsp water
2 tbsp rice vinegar
2 tbsp nam pla (Thai fish sauce)
3 tbsp white sugar, preferably caster (superfine)
1 small carrot, peeled and cut into thin shreds
grated zest and juice of 1 small lime
1 garlic clove, crushed
1 tsp light soy sauce
handful of coriander (cilantro), finely chopped
2 fresh red chillies, finely diced

1 Put the water, rice vinegar, nam pla and sugar in a small saucepan. Set over a medium heat and stir until the sugar dissolves.

2 Bring to the boil, then remove the pan from the heat and stir in the carrot. Set aside to cool.

3 When the sauce is cool, stir in the lime zest and juice, garlic, soy sauce, coriander and chillies. Transfer to a small bowl before serving.

OR YOU CAN TRY THIS...
– Add some grated fresh root ginger.
– Stir in some finely sliced spring onion (scallion).

MEXICAN HOT SAUCE

MAKES: APPROX. 240ML/8FL OZ (1 CUP) | **PREP:** 15 MINUTES | **STAND:** 2–6 DAYS

225g/8oz fresh green or red jalapeño chillies, halved
1 tsp sea salt crystals
150ml/5fl oz (⅔ cup) white vinegar
2 garlic cloves, crushed
1 tsp soft light brown sugar

To make an authentic-tasting Mexican sauce you need to use the right chillies. You can now buy fresh or dried jalapeño, ancho, Serrano, guajillo, habanero and poblano chillies, plus many other varieties, online or by mail order as well as from some supermarkets and specialist stores. You can adjust the number of chillies used in these recipes according to how much heat you like. Serve these sauces with tacos, burritos, enchiladas, tamales or fajitas, or simply drizzle over some chilli-fried eggs and sliced avocado.

1 Put the chillies and salt in a food processor or chopper and blitz briefly to a paste.

2 Transfer to a large clean screwtop jar or a Mason glass jar. Seal with the lid and set aside overnight or for 12 hours at room temperature. The chillies will start to ferment.

3 Add the vinegar and give everything a good stir. Seal with the lid and leave at room temperature for at least 24 hours. For a really intense taste, you can leave it for longer – up to 5 days.

4 Transfer to a blender or food processor and add the garlic and sugar. Blitz until smooth and then pass through a fine sieve, pressing down with a spoon, into a bowl below.

5 Decant into a sterilized 250ml/8fl oz jar or bottle (see tip below). You can eat it straight away and store in the fridge for up to 3 months.

TIP: Wash jars and lids in hot soapy water, then place them on a baking tray (cookie sheet) and put in an oven preheated to 140°C, 275°F, gas mark 1 for about 15 minutes.

SWEET THAI CHILLI SAUCE

MAKES: 300ML/½ PINT (1¼ CUPS) | **PREP:** 10 MINUTES | **COOK:** 15 MINUTES

5 long fresh red chillies,
  halved
6 garlic cloves, peeled
2.5cm/1in piece fresh root
  ginger, peeled and sliced
grated zest and juice of
  2 limes
4 tbsp water
200g/7oz (scant 1 cup)
  white sugar
100ml/3½fl oz (generous
  ⅓ cup) rice vinegar
3 tbsp nam pla
  (Thai fish sauce)

It's fun to make your own sweet chilli sauce at home, and it's surprisingly quick and easy to do, too. It should be stored in a screwtop jar, but sterilize it first by washing it out thoroughly and rinsing it well, then place on the shelf of a preheated oven set to 140°C, 275°F, gas mark 1 and leave for 20–30 minutes until dry.

1 Put the chillies, garlic, ginger, lime zest and juice in a blender or food chopper and blitz to a thick paste.

2 Put the water and sugar in a deep, heavy-based saucepan and set over a low to medium heat. Stir gently until all the sugar has dissolved, then turn up the heat and boil until the syrup starts to change colour and turn golden evenly all over. Watch carefully so it doesn't burn!

3 As soon as it starts to change colour and smell like caramel, quickly add the vinegar, nam pla and the chilli and garlic mixture – don't stand too close to the pan as it will spit – then reduce the heat.

4 Simmer gently for 4–5 minutes, then remove from the heat and set aside to cool a little. If you want the sauce thicker, simmer it for a little longer.

5 Pour the sauce into a 300ml/½ pint sterilized airtight jar (see page 13), cover with a wax disc and screw on the lid. Store for up to 2 months in a cool dry place or keep in the fridge.

OR YOU CAN TRY THIS...
– If you want a milder-tasting sauce, deseed a couple of the chillies before chopping.
– If you like really intense heat, use extra hot chillies and add a pinch of dried crushed chilli flakes or ½ teaspoon cayenne pepper.

HOME-MADE FERMENTED SRIRACHA

MAKES: APPROX. 300ML/½ PINT (1¼ CUPS) | **PREP:** 20 MINUTES | **FERMENT:** 5 DAYS
COOK: 20 MINUTES

200g/7oz fresh hot red
   chillies, chopped
150g/5oz red (bell) peppers,
   deseeded and chopped
4 garlic cloves, peeled
60g/2oz palm sugar
1 tsp sea salt (flakes or
   crystals)
1 tbsp nam pla
   (Thai fish sauce)
2 tbsp rice vinegar

**Sriracha has gone from a little-known hot chilli sauce to a global
gastronomic phenomenon in just a few years. Here's a recipe you
can make yourself at home – if you don't want to wait while it
ferments, try the quick version opposite.**

1 Blitz the chillies, red peppers, garlic, sugar and salt in a blender,
   food processor or food chopper until you have a coarse paste.

2 Transfer the mixture to a glass bowl and cover with cling film
   (plastic wrap). Set aside at room temperature (not in the fridge)
   for about 2 days until it starts to ferment and bubbles appear.

3 Uncover and stir the mixture, then cover again with cling film.
   Repeat this once every 24 hours for 3 more days.

4 Pour the fermented mixture into a blender and blitz until smooth,
   then strain through a fine sieve, pushing it through with a spoon,
   into a small saucepan.

5 Add the nam pla and rice vinegar and bring to the boil. Reduce
   the heat and let the sauce bubble away (not too gentle a simmer)
   for 10–15 minutes or until it reduces and thickens. Remove the pan
   from the heat and leave to cool.

6 Transfer to 350ml/12fl oz sterilized jar or bottles (see page 13),
   then cover with a seal or screwtop lid. Store in a cool, dark place.
   After opening, it will stay fresh in the fridge for up to 4 weeks.

OR YOU CAN TRY THIS...
– If you don't have palm sugar, use soft light brown sugar or even
   granulated instead.
– You can substitute any white vinegar for the rice vinegar.

QUICK SAUCES

QUICK SRIRACHA

MAKES: APPROX. 300ML/½ PINT (1¼ CUPS)
PREP: 10 MINUTES | **COOK:** 10 MINUTES

225g/8oz fresh hot red chillies, chopped
4 garlic cloves, peeled
1 tsp sea salt (flakes or crystals)
2 tbsp palm sugar
45ml/3 tbsp rice vinegar
90ml/3½fl oz (generous ⅓ cup) water
1 tsp nam pla (Thai fish sauce)

1 Put all the ingredients in a heavy-based saucepan and set over a low-medium heat. Stir until the sugar dissolves.

2 Increase the heat and bring to the boil. Reduce the heat and let the sauce bubble away (not too gentle a simmer) for 5 minutes. Remove the pan from the heat and leave to cool.

3 When it's tepid (at room temperature), blitz the sauce in a blender until it's really smooth and free from any lumps.

4 Pour through a fine sieve into a bowl, pressing down firmly with a spoon to push the liquid through.

5 Transfer to a 300ml/½ pint sterilized jar (see page 13) and cover with a seal or screwtop lid. This will keep in the fridge for up to 4 weeks.

QUICK JALAPEÑO SAUCE

MAKES: APPROX. 600ML/1 PINT (2½ CUPS)
PREP: 15 MINUTES | **COOK:** 25 MINUTES

1 tsp olive oil
300g/10oz fresh green or red jalapeño
  chillies, deseeded and sliced
4 garlic cloves, crushed
1 small onion, finely chopped
pinch of sea salt
360ml/12fl oz (1½ cups) water
150ml/5fl oz (⅔ cup) white vinegar

1 Heat the olive oil in a saucepan set over a medium-high heat. Add the chillies, garlic and onion and cook for 4–5 minutes.

2 Stir in the salt and water and let the sauce bubble away over a medium-high heat for about 20 minutes until the onion and chillies are really soft and the liquid reduces a little. Stir from time to time to stop it sticking to the pan. Set aside to cool.

3 Transfer to a blender or food processor and add the vinegar. Blitz until you have a smooth sauce.

4 Pour into sterilized screwtop jars or bottles (see page 13) and chill in the fridge. This will keep well in the fridge for about 3 months.

OR YOU CAN TRY THIS...
– Add a good pinch of ground cumin.
– Add a spoonful of sugar if you have a sweet tooth.

HARISSA

MAKES: 1 SMALL JAR | **PREP:** 15 MINUTES | **COOK:** 15–20 MINUTES

10 fresh red chillies
1 large red (bell) pepper
½ tsp coriander seeds
½ tsp caraway seeds
½ tsp cumin seeds
3 garlic cloves, chopped
½ tsp sea salt flakes
2 tsp tomato purée (paste)
1 tbsp lemon juice
1 tbsp olive oil, plus extra
    for preserving
½ tsp finely diced preserved
    lemon skin

**ROSE HARISSA
VARIATION:**
Omit the lemon and add
¼–½ tsp rose water and a
few fragrant fresh rose petals
to the blender. Only use rose
petals from the garden that
haven't been sprayed with
pesticides.

This fiery bright red sauce, which is sometimes thick like a paste, is eaten widely throughout North Africa. Fragrant and spicy, you need only a small amount, especially if you're using it as a flavouring for stews, tagines, soups, sauces and couscous. Or you can serve it like the locals do in Morocco: put a spoonful in a small bowl, pour over some good fruity olive oil and dip hunks of bread into it.

1 Preheat the oven to 220°C, 425°F, gas mark 7.

2 Put the chillies and red pepper on a baking tray (cookie sheet) and roast in the preheated oven for 15–20 minutes or until soft and the skin is starting to char and blister. Alternatively, pop them under a hot grill (broiler) for a few minutes, turning occasionally, until blistered and blackened all over.

3 Put the chillies and red pepper in a plastic bag, seal, and set aside to steam until cool enough to handle. Peel away and discard the skin of the peppers and then the chillies – wearing gloves for these. Put the flesh and seeds of the chillies, and the flesh only of the pepper (discard the seeds) in a food processor or food chopper.

4 Heat a small dry frying pan (skillet) and add the spice seeds. Toast, tossing gently, for 1–2 minutes until they start to release their aroma. Take care that they don't burn. Grind to a powder with a pestle and mortar, then add to the chillies and red pepper.

5 Add the garlic, salt, tomato purée, lemon juice and oil, then blitz to a smooth paste. Check the flavour, adding the lemon skin and more salt or lemon if needed.

6 Transfer to a sterilized screwtop jar (see page 13) and top with a little layer of olive oil, which acts as a natural preservative. Seal and store in the fridge, where it will keep well for about 2 weeks.

– For an even more fiery flavour, soak 1–2 dried ancho and/or chipotle chillies in boiling water until softened. Discard the stems and seeds and blitz the flesh with the other ingredients.
– Add some crushed dried chilli flakes.
– Sauté a finely chopped small red onion in a little oil until tender and then blitz with the other ingredients.
– For a smoky flavour, add ½–1 tsp smoked paprika.
– You can cool the harissa and serve it as an attractive marbled dip by stirring a little into a bowl of natural yoghurt.

GREEN HARISSA

MAKES: APPROX. 210ML/7FL OZ (SCANT 1 CUP) | **PREP:** 15 MINUTES

1 tbsp cumin seeds
2 tsp coriander seeds
good pinch of ground
    cinnamon
100g/3½oz (1 cup) chopped
    spinach leaves
2 spring onions (scallions),
    chopped
1 large bunch of coriander
    (cilantro), chopped
    (leaves and stalks)
handful of mint or flat-leaf
    parsley, chopped
4 garlic cloves, crushed
4 fresh green chillies, halved
juice of 1 lemon
½ tsp sea salt crystals
60ml/2fl oz (¼ cup) olive oil
freshly ground black pepper

1 Set a small dry frying pan (skillet) over a medium heat. Add the spice seeds to the hot pan and toast, tossing gently, for about 2 minutes until fragrant. Take care that they don't burn. Remove from the pan and allow to cool.

2 Put the cooled toasted seeds in a blender or food processor and pulse until finely ground. Add the cinnamon, spinach, spring onions, herbs, garlic, chillies, lemon juice and salt. Blitz for a few seconds and then slowly add the olive oil through the feed tube with the motor running. Blitz until smooth and free from any large lumps.

3 Season to taste with black pepper and transfer to a bowl or 250ml/ 8fl oz screwtop jar. Cover and chill in the fridge. The harissa will keep for 4–5 days.

OR YOU CAN TRY THIS...
– Add some rocket leaves (arugula) or chopped kale.
– Roast or grill the chillies and remove the skins for a more smoky flavour.
– Add some preserved lemon.

SZECHUAN HOT PLUM SAUCE

MAKES: APPROX. 6 x 600ML/1 PINT JARS | **PREP:** 20 MINUTES | **COOK:** 1½ HOURS

1.3kg/3lb ripe plums, stoned (pitted) and quartered

450g/1lb apples, peeled, cored and cut into chunks

2 red onions, finely chopped

1 red (bell) pepper, deseeded and diced

3 fresh red chillies, diced

5 garlic cloves, crushed

240ml/8fl oz (1 cup) water

900g/2lb (4½ cups) light brown sugar

720ml/1¼ pints (3 cups) rice vinegar

60ml/2fl oz (¼ cup) light soy sauce

5cm/2in piece fresh root ginger, peeled and sliced into fine splinters

2 star anise

1 tsp Sichuan peppercorns, crushed

2 tsp five-spice powder

1 cinnamon stick, broken in half

This spicy sauce tastes delicious with pies, cold meat and cheese, or you can spoon it over chicken breasts before baking them in the oven to give them an appetising and delicious glaze. If you have a plum tree in your garden, this is a great way to use up windfalls.

1 Put the plums, apples, red onions, red pepper, chillies and garlic in a large heavy-based preserving pan (or saucepan) with the water. Bring to the boil, then reduce the heat and simmer for 5–10 minutes or so until everything starts to soften.

2 Add the sugar and stir with a wooden spoon until it dissolves. Add the vinegar, soy sauce, ginger and spices.

3 Turn up the heat and when the liquid is boiling, reduce the temperature slightly. Let the sauce bubble away for 1–1¼ hours (if it takes longer, don't worry) or until it reduces and is thick and slightly glossy. Remove from the heat and take out the cinnamon stick.

4 Ladle the hot sauce into sterilized jars (see page 13), cover with a disc of waxed paper and seal. Leave to cool then store in a cool, dry place. The sauce will keep well for several months, unopened. Once opened, keep in the fridge for up to 1 month.

OR YOU CAN TRY THIS...

– For more heat, add a good pinch of crushed dried chilli flakes.
– Make it spicier with some whole or ground cloves and a good grinding of black pepper.
– If you don't have rice vinegar, substitute red wine or cider vinegar.

TOMATO CHILLI JAM

MAKES: APPROX. 1.3KG/3LB | **PREP:** 15 MINUTES | **COOK:** 1 HOUR

1kg/2lb 3oz ripe tomatoes

4 garlic cloves, peeled

5cm/2in piece fresh root ginger, peeled and chopped

3–4 large fresh red chillies, halved

45ml (3 tbsp) nam pla (Thai fish sauce)

600g/1lb 5oz (3 cups) granulated sugar

240ml/8fl oz (1 cup) red wine vinegar or cider vinegar

TIP: Don't add salt. The nam pla is very salty and will do the trick.

When tomatoes are in season and plentiful, this is a great way of using them up. Tomato chilli jam is easy to make and is seriously addictive! Serve it with cheese and crackers, cold chicken, charcuterie, roasted vegetables or anything you fancy.

1 Put half the tomatoes in a food processor with the garlic, ginger, chillies and nam pla. Blitz to a purée, then transfer to a preserving pan or a large heavy-based saucepan.

2 Chop the remaining tomatoes into small pieces and set aside.

3 Add the sugar and vinegar to the tomato mixture in the pan. Stir over a low-medium heat until the sugar dissolves. Turn up the heat and bring to the boil.

4 Reduce the heat and add the chopped tomatoes. Simmer for about 45 minutes, stirring occasionally to prevent it sticking to the bottom of the pan, until the mixture reduces and thickens (don't worry if it takes longer).

5 Pour the hot tomato chilli jam into sterilized jars (see page 13), then cover with waxed paper discs and lids or cellophane covers.

6 Store in a cool, dry place. It will keep for up to 12 months. Once opened, keep in the fridge for up to 1 month.

OR YOU CAN TRY THIS...

– Add a couple of whole star anise to the pan while the jam is cooking.

– Use light brown sugar instead of white.

– For a milder jam, deseed all or 2 of the chillies.

– Try rice wine vinegar or white wine vinegar.

– Add some crushed toasted cumin and coriander seeds.

WEST INDIAN HOT PEPPER SAUCE

MAKES: APPROX. 250ML/8FL OZ (1 CUP) | **PREP:** 15 MINUTES | **COOK:** 20–25 MINUTES

1 tbsp vegetable oil
4 Scotch bonnet chilli
    peppers, halved
3 garlic cloves, peeled
1 onion, roughly chopped
125g/4oz (½ cup) chopped
    papaya or mango
juice of 1 lime
60ml/2fl oz (¼ cup) white
    vinegar
2 tbsp light brown sugar
good pinch of ground cumin
1 tsp mustard
small bunch of coriander
    (cilantro), finely chopped
salt and freshly ground
    black pepper

TIP: For an even speedier, raw version of this sauce, blitz the chillies, garlic, onion and mango in a blender or food chopper, then add the remaining ingredients and blitz again. Check the seasoning and store in a screwtop jar in the fridge. This will keep for 3–4 days.

The addition of fruit makes this fiery hot sauce deliciously sweet. Every Caribbean island has its own special pepper sauce and traditionally they were made by hand in a food mill. Nowadays a blender does the hard work for you. Take care here, as Scotch bonnet chillies are fearsomely hot. Wear gloves and don't rub your eyes, mouth or skin when handling them. This makes a great dipping sauce for grilled chicken, fish and vegetables.

1 Heat the oil in a saucepan over a low-medium heat. Add the chillies, garlic and onion and cook gently for about 5 minutes until softened.

2 Transfer to a blender or food chopper and blitz to a paste. Add the fruit, lime juice, vinegar, sugar, cumin and mustard, and blitz until smooth.

3 Pour into a saucepan and bring to the boil. Reduce the heat and simmer for 15–20 minutes until the sauce reduces and thickens. Stir in the coriander.

4 Check the seasoning and pour into a 250ml/8fl oz screwtop jar. Leave to cool, then seal and store in the fridge. This will keep well for 4–5 days.

OR YOU CAN TRY THIS...
– Use diced pineapple.
– Habanero chillies can be substituted for the Scotch bonnets.
– Add some grated lime zest.
– Use spring onions (scallions).

SNACKS

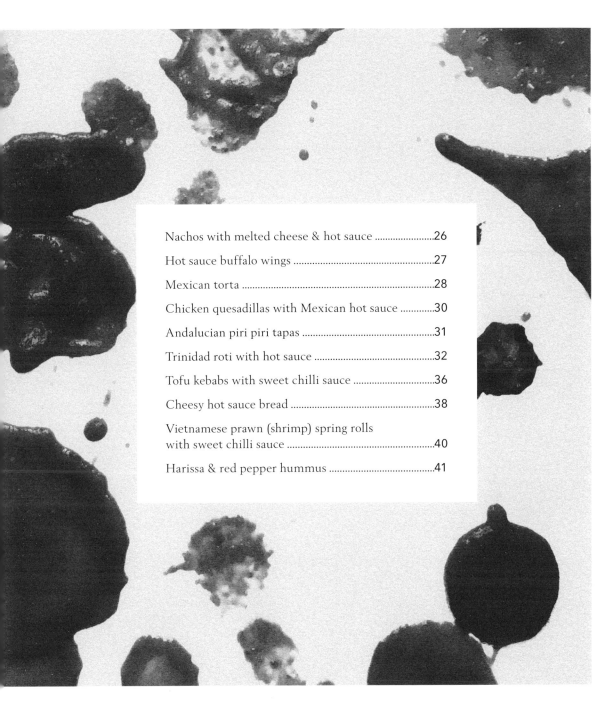

NACHOS WITH MELTED CHEESE & HOT SAUCE

SERVES: 4 | **PREP:** 10 MINUTES | **COOK:** 10 MINUTES

225g/8oz salted corn
    tortilla chips
4 tomatoes, deseeded
    and diced
1 x 400g/14oz can (2 cups)
    kidney beans, rinsed and
    drained
1 bunch spring onions
    (scallions), finely sliced
4 pickled jalapeños, thinly
    sliced
100g/3½oz (¾ cup) grated
    Cheddar cheese
150g/5oz (1 cup) hot salsa
    or pico de gallo
150g/5oz (1 cup) guacamole
Mexican hot sauce, for
    drizzling

Nachos are great as a snack or served pre-dinner or as part of a hot buffet. If you top the tortilla chips with chilli con carne (made with minced beef) you can even serve them as a main course. Any Mexican hot sauce can be sprinkled over them at the end as a finishing touch and to add the heat you crave.

1 Preheat the oven to 200°C, 400°F, gas mark 6.

2 Put the tortilla chips in a large ovenproof dish and scatter the tomatoes, kidney beans, spring onions and jalapeños over the top. Sprinkle with the grated cheese.

3 Bake in the preheated oven for about 10 minutes or until hot and the cheese has melted and is bubbling.

4 Spoon the salsa (or pico de gallo) and guacamole over the top and drizzle with hot sauce. Serve immediately.

OR YOU CAN TRY THIS...

– Instead of the pickled jalapeños, use 2 sliced fresh red or green chillies.
– For a light lunch, spoon some chilli con carne – made with minced (ground) beef and kidney beans – over the nachos. Sprinkle with cheese and cook in the oven for 10–15 minutes. Serve as above with salsa, guacamole and hot sauce.
– Use grated Monterey Jack cheese instead of Cheddar.
– Sprinkle with chopped coriander (cilantro).
– Add a dollop of sour cream before serving.
– Instead of guacamole, scatter with diced avocado tossed in lime juice.

HOT SAUCE BUFFALO WINGS

SERVES: 4 | **PREP:** 10 MINUTES | **MARINATE:** 2 HOURS MINIMUM | **COOK:** 30 MINUTES

spray oil
8 chicken wings, cut in
2 (16 wing pieces)
1 tsp smoked paprika
½ tsp ground cumin
½ tsp ground coriander
pinch of dried thyme
1 tbsp grated fresh root
ginger
60ml/2fl oz (4 tbsp)
hot pepper sauce
2 tbsp clear honey
freshly ground black
pepper

Sriracha yoghurt dip:
240g/8½oz (1 cup)
0%-fat Greek yoghurt
2–3 tbsp Sriracha
few chives, snipped

You can use literally any hot sauce to make these spicy chicken wings. We've stirred some Sriracha into a cooling bowl of yoghurt for a dip, but you could use plain yoghurt, sour cream or some tzatziki instead.

1 Put the chicken wings in a bowl and spray lightly with oil.

2 Mix together the ground spices, thyme, ginger, hot pepper sauce and honey. Grind in some black pepper and pour the sauce over the chicken wings. Turn them in the mixture to cover them completely. Cover the bowl with a lid or some cling film (plastic wrap) and leave to marinate in the fridge for at least 2 hours – overnight, if wished.

3 When you're ready to cook the buffalo wings, preheat the oven to 200°C, 400°F, gas mark 6. Line a large baking sheet (cookie tray) with kitchen foil and lightly spray with oil.

4 Arrange the chicken wings in a single layer on the lined baking sheet, spooning over any leftover marinade. Bake in the preheated oven for about 30 minutes, turning them and coating with the marinade, until the wings are sticky, well glazed and a deep golden brown.

5 Meanwhile, make the Sriracha yoghurt dip: spoon the yoghurt into a serving bowl and swirl in the Sriracha to make an attractive pattern on top. Sprinkle with chives and a grinding of black pepper.

6 Serve the buffalo wings as a snack or pre-dinner appetizer with the dip.

OR YOU CAN TRY THIS...

– Vary the spices in the marinade: try chilli powder, cayenne, regular paprika or some ground toasted fennel seeds.
– Add some crushed garlic to the marinade, or some seedy mustard, lemon zest and juice.
– Use boned chicken thighs instead of wings.

MEXICAN TORTA

SERVES: 4 | **PREP:** 15 MINUTES | **COOK:** 15 MINUTES

2 whole red (bell) peppers
olive oil spray
2 courgettes (zucchini), sliced
200g/7oz chorizo sausages,
    sliced
4 large, flat crusty rolls
1 avocado, halved, stoned
    (pitted) and peeled
juice of ½ lime
4 heaped tbsp canned
    refried beans
1 large ripe tomato, sliced
½ red onion, finely sliced
few crisp lettuce leaves,
    e.g. cos (romaine)
Mexican hot sauce,
    for drizzling

Chilli mayo:
4 heaped tbsp light
    mayonnaise
1 tbsp chipotle chilli sauce
    or Tabasco
grated zest and juice of
    ½ lime

In Mexico, a 'torta' is a thick wedge of a sandwich with more filling than bread. You can put virtually anything in it, just make sure you drizzle with plenty of hot sauce!

1 Make the chilli mayo: mix all the ingredients together in a bowl.

2 Pop the red peppers under a hot grill (broiler), turning them occasionally, until the skin is blistered all over. Put them in a plastic bag and set aside until cool enough to handle. Peel away and discard the skin and seeds. Cut the flesh into large pieces and set aside.

3 Lightly spray a griddle (grill) pan with oil (a few squirts is enough) and set over a medium heat. Cook the courgettes for a few minutes each side until tender and golden brown. Remove and set aside.

4 Turn up the heat and add the chorizo to the hot pan. Cook for about 3 minutes on each side until crisp and golden brown. Remove and drain on kitchen paper (paper towels).

5 Cut the rolls in half and toast them on the griddle pan in the fat that's oozed out of the chorizo.

6 Mash the avocado with the lime juice and smear over one half of each toasted roll and top with the pepper and courgette slices. Spread the other half with the chilli mayo.

7 Add the refried beans, chorizo, sliced tomato, onion and lettuce, and drizzle with the hot sauce. Cover with the other half of each roll that's been spread with chilli mayo.

8 Press down on top of each torta, cut in half and enjoy!

OR YOU CAN TRY THIS...
– Use some fresh or bottled hot salsa instead of fresh sliced tomatoes.
– Add some sliced or grated hard cheese, e.g. Cheddar or Monterey Jack, or some queso fresco (Mexican soft cheese) or crumbled feta.

CHICKEN QUESADILLAS WITH MEXICAN HOT SAUCE

SERVES: 4 | **PREP:** 15 MINUTES | **COOK:** 12–16 MINUTES

200g/7oz (1¾ cups) grated Cheddar cheese
6 spring onions (scallions), thinly sliced
1 fresh red chilli, diced
1 small bunch of coriander (cilantro), chopped
1 ripe avocado, stoned (pitted), peeled and diced
juice of 1 lime
225g/8oz skinned cooked chicken breast, shredded
4 large flour tortillas
spray olive oil
salt and freshly ground black pepper
Mexican hot sauce, for drizzling
salsa and sour cream or yoghurt, to serve

These are the Mexican equivalent of toasted cheese sandwiches, and they are just as simple to make. If wished, you can divide the filling between the tortillas, spreading it over one half, and folding it over to make a half-moon shape. Press down on the edges and cook as directed below.

1 In a bowl, mix together the grated cheese, spring onions, chilli and coriander. Season lightly with salt and pepper.

2 Sprinkle the avocado with the lime juice and add to the cheesy mixture with the chicken. Mix well.

3 Divide the mixture between 2 tortillas but not right up to the edges – leave a thin border around each one. Place the other tortilla on top and press the halves firmly together.

4 Lightly spray a large non-stick frying pan (skillet) with oil and set over a medium heat. When it's really hot, carefully add one of the quesadillas and cook for 3–4 minutes until golden underneath. Use a spatula to flip it over and cook the other side for a couple of minutes, keeping an eye on it to check it doesn't burn. The filling should be heated through and the cheese melting. Slide the quesadilla out of the pan and keep warm while you cook the other one.

5 To serve, cut each quesadilla into 6 wedges. Drizzle with hot sauce and eat immediately with some salsa and sour cream or yoghurt.

OR YOU CAN TRY THIS...

– Instead of chicken, use some diced ham, chorizo, cooked pancetta cubes or bacon lardons.
– Use bottled jalapeño chillies or some hot sauce instead of a fresh chilli.
– Vegetarians can use refried beans instead of chicken.
– Instead of Cheddar, try Monterey Jack, Gruyère or grated mozzarella.

ANDALUCIAN PIRI PIRI TAPAS

SERVES: 4 | **PREP:** 10 MINUTES | **COOK:** 10 MINUTES

6 tbsp olive oil
1 tbsp paprika
pinch of crushed dried chilli
    flakes
few drops of piri piri sauce
3–4 garlic cloves, crushed
small bunch of flat-leaf
    parsley, finely chopped
16 peeled raw king prawns
    (jumbo shrimp)
crusty bread, to serve

A small dish of sizzling prawns in hot garlicky olive oil with spices and herbs can be found in every tapas bar in Andalucia. Add a dash of piri piri hot sauce and use some crusty bread to mop up the fragrant juices. Delicious! Wash it down with a glass of chilled Manzanilla sherry and it's even better. In Spain this is known as *gambas pil pil* or *gambas al ajillo*.

1 Preheat the oven to 220°C, 425°F, gas mark 7.

2 Divide the oil between 4 individual ramekin dishes (the Spanish use shallow terracotta ones). Pop into the oven for 4–5 minutes until the oil is really hot.

3 Stir the paprika, chilli flakes, piri piri sauce, garlic and most of the parsley into the hot oil and then divide the prawns between the 4 dishes.

4 Cook in the oven for about 5 minutes until the prawns turn pink all over and the oil is sizzling.

5 Sprinkle with the rest of the parsley and serve piping hot with crusty bread.

OR YOU CAN TRY THIS...
– Add some finely chopped onion or spring onions (scallions).
– Use small prawns (shrimp) instead of large ones – you'll need about 300g/10oz.
– Substitute smoked paprika for the regular sort.
– Double the quantity and serve as a light lunch with a tomato salad.
– Use diced fresh red chillies instead of dried flakes and hot sauce.

TRINIDAD ROTI WITH HOT SAUCE

SERVES: 4 | **PREP:** 30 MINUTES | **REST:** 1 HOUR | **COOK:** 45 MINUTES

225g/8oz (scant 2 cups)
   self-raising (self-rising)
   flour, sifted
good pinch of ground
   turmeric
½ tsp salt
1 tbsp sunflower oil,
   plus extra for brushing
   and frying
120ml/4fl oz (½ cup)
   tepid water
West Indian hot sauce,
   to serve

Roti are a popular snack and street food throughout the West Indies, or you can serve them as a light meal with some fried plantains and rice. Every Caribbean island has its own versions of spicy hot pepper sauce – Habanero chillies, scorpion peppers and Scotch bonnets are often used in Trinidad and Tobago. You can now buy many of these hot sauces online and experience their serious heat in your own home.

1 Make the roti dough: put the flour, turmeric and salt in a mixing bowl and drizzle the oil over the top. Mix in the water, a little at a time, until you have a soft dough. If it's too dry, add a little more water.

2 Knead the dough lightly for a few minutes, then cover and set aside to rest for at least 30 minutes.

3 Divide the dough into 8 equal-sized pieces and use a rolling pin to roll each one out into a thin circle. Lightly brush half of each circle with oil and fold over. Brush half of the semicircle with oil and fold over again into a quarter. Set aside for 30 minutes again.

4 Meanwhile, make the filling: heat the oil in a heavy-based frying pan (skillet) and cook the onion and garlic over a low-medium heat for 5 minutes. Add the sweet potato and chicken and cook for 5 minutes, stirring occasionally, until the chicken is browned all over. Stir in the curry powder and allspice.

*Sweet potato and
  chicken filling:*
2 tbsp sunflower oil
1 onion, finely chopped
2 garlic cloves, crushed
1 large sweet potato,
  peeled and diced
300g/10oz chicken breast
  fillets, diced
1 tbsp curry powder
good pinch of ground
  allspice
120ml/4fl oz (½ cup)
  coconut milk
100g/3½oz baby spinach
  leaves
salt and freshly ground
  black pepper

5 Add the coconut milk and simmer for about 15 minutes until the
vegetables are tender and the liquid has evaporated. A couple of
minutes before the end of the cooking time, stir in the spinach
and season to taste.

6 Roll out the roti into thin circles and fry, one at a time, in a little
hot oil in a frying pan for 2–3 minutes until golden brown underneath
and puffy, then flip over and cook the other side. Drain on kitchen
paper (paper towels) and keep warm.

7 Divide the filling between the roti pancakes and fold over or roll up.
Serve immediately, drizzled with West Indian hot sauce.

OR YOU CAN TRY THIS...
– Cubed pumpkin or butternut squash can be substituted for
  sweet potato.
– Use prawns (shrimp), pork or minced (ground) beef instead of chicken.
– Vegetarians can omit the chicken and add drained canned black beans.
– Use curry paste instead of curry powder.

TOFU KEBABS WITH SWEET CHILLI SAUCE

SERVES: 4 | **PREP:** 10 MINUTES | **MARINATE:** 30 MINUTES | **COOK:** 5 MINUTES

200g/7oz tofu, cubed
1 green (bell) pepper,
    deseeded and cut into
    chunks
1 red or yellow (bell)
    pepper, deseeded and
    cut into chunks
1 red onion, cut into wedges
spray olive oil
few sprigs of coriander
    (cilantro), chopped
sweet chilli sauce, for
    drizzling

Marinade:
2 tbsp light soy sauce
2 garlic cloves, crushed
1 tbsp tomato purée (paste)
1 tsp clear honey

Tofu, or bean curd, has a silky texture and is very high in protein, making it an extremely healthy food, especially for vegetarians. It has rather a bland, delicate flavour, so it's often marinated before cooking and added to spicy dishes or served with a hot sauce.

1 Mix together the marinade ingredients in a small bowl. Add the tofu and stir into the marinade until coated all over. Set aside for 30 minutes.

2 Thread the tofu, peppers and red onion alternately onto 4 long or 8 short skewers and spray them lightly with oil.

3 Cook on a hot griddle (grill) pan or barbecue or under a preheated grill (broiler) for about 5 minutes, turning the kebabs occasionally, until the vegetables are tender and slightly charred on the edges and the tofu is golden.

4 Serve immediately, sprinkled with coriander and drizzled with sweet chilli sauce.

OR YOU CAN TRY THIS...
– Use any hot sauce or dip into some harissa.
– Vary the vegetables: try courgette (zucchini) or aubergine (eggplant) chunks, button mushrooms or cherry tomatoes.
– Instead of tofu, use cubed halloumi cheese and drizzle with Sriracha.

CHEESY HOT SAUCE BREAD

MAKES: 1 LOAF | **PREP:** 30 MINUTES | **RISE:** 2 HOURS | **COOK:** 30 MINUTES

500g/1lb 2oz (4 cups) strong white bread flour, plus extra for dusting
1 tsp salt
15g/½oz (1 tbsp) butter, diced
1 tsp sugar
14g/½oz (2 tsp) easy-blend (easy-bake) yeast
60ml/2fl oz (¼ cup) milk
170ml/6fl oz (¾ cup) water
oil, for greasing
milk or beaten egg, for glazing

Cheesy hot sauce swirl:
4 tbsp hot sauce, e.g. Sriracha or Mexican smoky chipotle sauce
100g/3½oz (1 cup) grated Cheddar cheese
1 bunch of chives, snipped

There is nothing more wonderful than the aroma of freshly baked bread, and who would have thought you could spice up a single loaf with some hot sauce? Breadmaking takes a little time but is well worth the effort – it's enjoyable, therapeutic as you roll, stretch and thump the dough, and surprisingly easy.

1 Sift the flour and salt into a large mixing bowl and rub in the butter with your fingertips. Stir in the sugar and yeast. Heat the milk and water until hand-hot, then mix into the flour to form a soft dough.

2 Turn out onto a lightly floured surface and knead for 5–10 minutes until the dough is elastic and smooth. Place in a lightly oiled bowl, cover with a clean cloth or cling film (plastic wrap) and leave in a warm place for about 1 hour until well risen and doubled in size.

3 Knock the dough down with your fists and roll out to a rectangle. Spread the hot sauce over the dough and sprinkle with the grated cheese and chives. Roll up and pat into a loaf. Place in a greased loaf tin (pan), cover and leave in a warm place for 30–60 minutes until it rises above the top of the tin.

4 Meanwhile, preheat the oven to 220°C, 425°F, gas mark 7.

5 Brush the top of the loaf with a little milk or beaten egg and bake in the preheated oven for about 30 minutes until golden brown. To test the loaf, tap the bottom – it will sound hollow when it's cooked.

6 Remove the loaf from the tin and cool on a wire rack. Cut into slices to serve and expose the wonderful red swirl.

OR YOU CAN TRY THIS...

– Double up on the ingredients and make 2 loaves. When cool, pop one into a freezer bag and freeze for up to 1 month.
– For a green swirl, use green Tabasco and add more chopped herbs, such as parsley, coriander (cilantro), thyme and oregano.

VIETNAMESE PRAWN (SHRIMP) SPRING ROLLS WITH SWEET CHILLI SAUCE

MAKES: 8 | **PREP:** 20 MINUTES | **COOK:** 5 MINUTES

1 tbsp sunflower oil
2 red (bell) peppers, deseeded and diced
1 large carrot, cut into small thin matchsticks
2.5cm/1in piece fresh root ginger, diced
100g/3½oz spring greens, kale or spinach, shredded
100g/3½oz bean sprouts
300g/10oz cooked peeled prawns (shrimp)
4 tbsp soy sauce
handful of coriander (cilantro), chopped
8 round rice paper wrappers
sweet chilli sauce, for dipping

These spring rolls are much fresher-tasting, lighter and healthier than the fried Chinese ones. The sweet chilli sauce enhances their delicate flavour. You can buy rice paper wrappings in oriental stores, delis and many supermarkets.

1 Heat the oil in a wok or large frying pan (skillet) over a high heat. Stir-fry the red peppers, carrot and ginger for 2 minutes, then add the greens, bean sprouts and prawns and stir-fry for 2 minutes. Stir in the soy sauce and coriander.

2 Fill a bowl with cold water and position it near you while you assemble the spring rolls.

3 Dip a rice paper wrapper into the water until it's pliable. Lay it out flat on a clean work surface and spoon some of the prawn and vegetable filling onto it, leaving a broad edge around it.

4 Fold the sides of the wrapper over the filling to enclose it and then roll up like a parcel. Repeat with the rest of the wrappers and filling.

5 Serve as snacks or appetizers with a bowl of sweet chilli sauce to dip.

OR YOU CAN TRY THIS...
– Use shredded cooked chicken or roast pork instead of prawns (shrimps).
– Vary the vegetables – try peas, spring onions (scallions), garlic and mushrooms.
– Add some rice vermicelli – follow the directions on the packet and mix into the filling.
– Substitute nam pla (Thai fish sauce) for the soy sauce – 2 tbsp will be enough.
– Make an alternative dip with soy sauce, sliced chillies and spring onions (scallions). Add a dash of lime juice and Sriracha to taste.

HARISSA & RED PEPPER HUMMUS

SERVES: 6 | **PREP:** 15 MINUTES | **COOK:** 5 MINUTES

2 red (bell) peppers
2 x 400g/14oz cans (3 cups) chickpeas
4 tbsp tahini
3–4 garlic cloves, crushed
juice of 1 large lemon
1–2 tsp harissa paste
olive oil, for drizzling
za'atar, paprika or sumac, for dusting
chopped parsley, for sprinkling
warm pitta bread, to serve

Hummus is easy to make if you use canned chickpeas. It tastes much better than the ready-made varieties you buy in supermarkets and delis. Serve as a snack with triangles of warm pitta bread or use as a dip for raw vegetable crudités. The grilled (broiled) red peppers lend a smoky flavour to this recipe, while the harissa adds heat and an intensity of colour.

1 Grill (broil) the red peppers under a preheated overhead grill (broiler), turning them occasionally, until softened and the skin is blistered and starting to char.

2 Pop them into a plastic bag, seal and leave to steam until cool enough to handle. Peel away and discard the skin and seeds. Cut the flesh into big pieces and place in a food processor or blender.

3 Drain the chickpeas, reserving the canning liquid, then rinse and set aside a few whole chickpeas for the garnish. Put the rest in the food processor or blender with the peppers.

4 Add the tahini, garlic and lemon juice. Blitz to a rough purée. Add a little of the reserved canning liquid and blitz until you end up with the desired consistency: a slightly grainy mixture which isn't too smooth nor too runny or stiff. Stir in the harissa to taste.

5 Transfer to a serving bowl, scatter the reserved chickpeas over the top and drizzle with olive oil. Dust lightly with za'atar, paprika or sumac and sprinkle with parsley. Serve with warm pitta bread.

NOTE: This will keep in the fridge for up to 3 days. Just store in an airtight container with a tightly fitting lid.

OR YOU CAN TRY THIS…
– Squeeze some fresh lemon juice over the top just before serving.
– Instead of grilling the peppers, use 1–2 tablespoons red pepper paste (available from some Middle Eastern delis and online).
– Add a tablespoon of pomegranate molasses for sweetness.
– Sprinkle with crushed dried chilli flakes.

BREAKFASTS
& BRUNCHES

JAMAICAN STAMP 'N' GO FISH FRITTERS

SERVES: 4 | **PREP:** 15 MINUTES | **SOAK:** OVERNIGHT (OR LONGER) | **COOK:** 30 MINUTES

225g/8oz salt cod, soaked
    in water overnight
200g/7oz self-raising
    (self-rising) flour
1 small red (bell) pepper,
    deseeded and diced
4 spring onions (scallions),
    finely sliced
1 tsp chopped fresh thyme
1 red Scotch bonnet chilli,
    deseeded and diced
freshly ground black pepper
vegetable oil, for shallow
    frying
West Indian hot pepper
    sauce, for drizzling
green bananas or plantains
    fried in coconut oil,
    to serve

CAUTION! Be careful
when frying the fritters.
Never leave the pan
unattended – keep an eye on
it as the oil will be very hot.

These crisp golden fritters are a Jamaican staple. They are eaten not only for breakfast but also as a snack throughout the day. Their name is derived from people stamping their feet impatiently as they wait in line for them at street stalls. When soaking the salt cod, change the water several times to get rid of the intense saltiness – the longer you soak it, the less salty it will be.

1 Rinse the salt cod thoroughly, changing the water several times. Pat dry with kitchen paper (paper towels), then cook in a pan of boiling water for about 20 minutes until tender and flaking. Drain well and break into small pieces, discarding the skin and any small bones.

2 Put the salt cod in a bowl with the flour, red pepper, spring onions, thyme, chilli and a grinding of black pepper. Mix well together, then stir in enough cold water to form a sticky mixture.

3 Heat some oil in a large frying pan (skillet) to a depth of 2cm over a medium-high heat. When it's sizzling hot, add a few spoonfuls of the salt cod mixture and fry until golden brown and crisp underneath. Turn the fritters over and cook the other side. Remove with a slotted spoon and drain on kitchen paper (paper towels). Keep warm while you cook the remaining fritters.

4 Serve the hot fritters with West Indian hot sauce and some green bananas or plantains fried in coconut oil.

OR YOU CAN TRY THIS...
– Use green (bell) pepper and green hot chillies.
– Add some chopped parsley or coriander (cilantro) to the mixture.
– Squeeze some fresh lime juice over the hot fritters.

MEXICAN BRUNCH

SERVES: 4 | **PREP:** 10 MINUTES | **COOK:** 40–45 MINUTES

4 large corn tortillas
2 tbsp vegetable oil
4 medium free-range eggs
pinch of crushed dried
    chilli flakes
small bunch of spring onions
    (scallions), thinly sliced
4 tbsp grated Cheddar or
    Monterey Jack cheese
2 ripe avocados, stoned
    (pitted), peeled and
    thinly sliced
Greek yoghurt, to serve

Hot tomato sauce:
2 tbsp olive oil
1 red onion, chopped
1 small red (bell) pepper,
    deseeded and diced
2 garlic cloves, crushed
1 fresh red chilli, diced
pinch of cumin seeds
2 x 400g/14oz cans
    chopped tomatoes
pinch of sugar
few drops of Tabasco
    or Mexican hot sauce
salt and freshly ground
    black pepper

This filling Mexican dish will keep you going throughout the day. You can make the hot tomato sauce in advance and reheat it for breakfast or brunch.

1 Make the hot tomato sauce: heat the olive oil in a large frying pan (skillet) over a low heat. Cook the red onion, red pepper, garlic and chilli for 8–10 minutes until tender.

2 Stir in the cumin seeds and cook for 1 minute, then add the tomatoes and simmer for 15–20 minutes, stirring occasionally, until the sauce reduces and thickens. Add the sugar and hot sauce to taste. Season with salt and pepper, if needed.

3 When you are ready to serve, heat the tortillas, one or two at a time, in a large dry frying pan (skillet), set over a low-medium heat, for 1–2 minutes each side – just long enough to make them golden and slightly crisp. Remove and keep warm.

4 Add the oil to the pan and fry the eggs over a high heat until the whites are set and crisp around the edges but the yolks are still runny. To set the film on top of the yolks, either spoon some hot oil over them or flash the pan under a hot grill (broiler).

5 Arrange the tortillas on 4 serving plates. Spoon over some hot tomato sauce and top with a fried egg. Scatter with the chilli flakes, spring onions, grated cheese and sliced avocado. Serve immediately with some Greek yoghurt on the side.

OR YOU CAN TRY THIS...
– Scatter some chopped coriander (cilantro) over the eggs.
– Add some diced chorizo or bacon to the tomato sauce.
– Serve with sour cream and guacamole.
– Flash under a hot grill (broiler) just before serving to melt the cheese.

CARIBBEAN CORN FRITTERS WITH HOT SAUCE

SERVES: 4 | **PREP:** 15 MINUTES | **COOK:** 10 MINUTES

225g/8oz (1 cup) canned sweetcorn kernels, drained
125g/4oz (1 cup) self-raising (self-rising) flour
½ tsp smoked paprika
2 medium free-range eggs, separated
1–2 tbsp milk
1 fresh red chilli, deseeded and diced
½ red onion, finely chopped
handful of coriander (cilantro), finely chopped
3 tbsp groundnut (peanut) oil
salt and freshly ground black pepper
West Indian hot sauce, for drizzling

Avocado salsa:
1 large ripe avocado, stoned (pitted), peeled and diced
3 juicy tomatoes, diced
½ red onion, diced
1 fresh green chilli, diced
2 garlic cloves, crushed
few sprigs of coriander (cilantro), chopped
juice of 1 lime

These healthy fritters are surprisingly easy to make and cook in just a few minutes. Serve them with fried or grilled (broiled) plantains or tomatoes, crispy bacon or fried eggs.

1 Make the avocado salsa: mix all the ingredients together in a bowl, then cover and set aside while you make the fritters.

2 Put the sweetcorn in a small pan and cover with a little water. Bring to the boil and cook for 2 minutes. Drain well.

3 Sift the flour into a bowl, add the smoked paprika, salt and pepper and make a well in the centre. In a separate bowl, whisk the egg yolks and milk and then beat in the seasoned flour until you have a stiff batter.

4 Whisk the egg whites until stiff in a clean, dry bowl. Using a metal spoon, fold the whites gently into the batter in a figure-of-eight movement. Gently stir in the sweetcorn, chilli, red onion and coriander, distributing them evenly.

5 Heat the oil in a non-stick frying pan (skillet) over a high heat. When it's really hot, add small spoonfuls of the sweetcorn batter, flattening them a little with a spatula, and cook in batches for about 2 minutes until golden brown underneath. Flip them over and cook until crisp and golden.

6 Serve the fritters, drizzled with hot sauce, with the avocado salsa.

OR YOU CAN TRY THIS...
– Use finely sliced spring onions (scallions) instead of red onion.
– Fry the fritters in sunflower or olive oil.
– If you're in a hurry, mix some diced avocado into a tub of bought ready-made salsa.
– Instead of a fresh chilli, use ½ tsp chipotle chilli flakes in the fritters.

TURKISH POACHED EGGS WITH HARISSA

SERVES: 4 | **PREP:** 5 MINUTES | **COOK:** 10 MINUTES

450g/1lb spinach
1 tbsp white wine vinegar
4 medium free-range eggs
60g/2oz (¼ cup) butter
1 tsp mild dried chilli flakes,
    e.g. Aleppo chilli
500g/1lb 2oz (2 cups)
    Greek yoghurt
3–4 garlic cloves, crushed
2 tsp harissa paste
few sprigs of dill, finely
    chopped
pitta or crusty bread,
    to serve

This dish of creamy poached eggs, delicately flavoured with dill and served with fiery harissa, is called *cilbir* in Turkey. It's served warm with pitta or hunks of bread to mop up the yoghurt and egg yolk.

1 Put the spinach in a large saucepan with a tablespoon of water. Cover with a lid and cook over a medium heat for about 2 minutes, shaking the pan occasionally, until the leaves wilt and turn bright green. Drain and keep warm.

2 Bring a pan of water to the boil. Add the vinegar and reduce the heat to a simmer. Gently crack the eggs, one at a time, into a bowl, and then slide into the simmering water. Poach for 3–4 minutes until the whites are set and the yolks are still runny. Remove carefully with a slotted spoon and drain on kitchen paper (paper towels).

3 Meanwhile, melt the butter in a small pan over a low-medium heat and whisk in the chilli flakes.

4 In another pan, heat the yoghurt and garlic very gently over the lowest possible heat, so the yoghurt doesn't separate.

5 Divide the spinach between 4 bowls and spoon the yoghurt over the top. Swirl in a little harissa. Top each bowl with a poached egg and pour over the melted butter. Sprinkle with dill and serve immediately with pitta or crusty bread.

OR YOU CAN TRY THIS...
– Leave out the spinach and add an extra poached egg to each bowl.
– Instead of chilli flakes, add a teaspoon of smoked paprika to the butter.
– Sprinkle some za'atar over the top with the dill.
– Instead of harissa, drizzle with your favourite hot sauce.

GREEN FRENCH TOAST WITH SWEET CHILLI SAUCE

SERVES: 4 | **PREP:** 5 MINUTES | **SOAK:** 2–3 MINUTES | **COOK:** 6 MINUTES

4 medium free-range eggs

90ml/3fl oz (scant ½ cup) milk

handful of parsley and chives, finely chopped

4 thin spring onions (scallions), finely sliced

4 medium slices wholemeal or seedy bread

spray olive oil

4 stems of cherry tomatoes on the vine

salt and freshly ground black pepper

sweet chilli sauce, for drizzling

We've got accustomed to French toast being sweet and served with fruit and maple syrup, but it's more colourful and even more delicious flavoured with onions and herbs. We've used sweet chilli sauce but any of your favourite hot sauces will work well.

1 Beat the eggs and milk together in a shallow bowl. Add the chopped herbs and spring onions. Season lightly with salt and pepper.

2 Place the bread in the eggy mixture and leave for 2–3 minutes to soak it up, turning the bread over to cover both sides.

3 Lightly spray a large non-stick frying pan (skillet) with oil and set over a low-medium heat. When the pan is hot, add the soaked bread, 1–2 slices at a time, and cook for 2–3 minutes until crisp and golden brown underneath. Turn them over and cook the other side. Keep warm while you cook the remaining French toast.

4 Meanwhile, cook the tomatoes in a hot griddle (grill) pan or under an overhead grill (broiler).

5 Serve the hot French toast, drizzled with sweet chilli sauce, with the grilled tomatoes.

OR YOU CAN TRY THIS...

– Add a pinch of ground cinnamon, allspice or nutmeg to the beaten egg mixture.
– Add some crushed garlic or vary the herbs: try some chopped basil, thyme or tarragon.
– Serve with crispy bacon, grilled (broiled) mushrooms or fried bananas.

SWEET POTATO PANCAKES WITH HOT SAUCE

SERVES: 4 | **PREP:** 15 MINUTES | **COOK:** 20–30 MINUTES

175g/6oz (1½ cups) plain (all-purpose) flour
1 tbsp baking powder
½ tsp salt
½ tsp freshly ground nutmeg
½ tsp ground cinnamon
2 medium free-range eggs, beaten
150ml/¼ pint (generous ½ cup) milk
60g/2oz (¼ cup) butter, melted, plus extra for frying
handful of coriander (cilantro), finely chopped
4 spring onions (scallions), thinly sliced
350g/12oz cooked sweet potato, mashed
crispy bacon rashers (slices), to serve
freshly ground black pepper
Sriracha or West Indian hot sauce, for drizzling

Use boiled, baked or microwaved sweet potatoes. The easiest way is to boil or bake them whole in their skins until tender. When they are cool enough to handle, peel off and discard the skins and mash the orange flesh inside.

1 Sift the flour, baking powder, salt and ground spices into a large mixing bowl.

2 In a separate bowl, beat together the eggs, milk and melted butter. Stir in the coriander, spring onions and mashed sweet potato until well combined. Add to the flour mixture, mixing well to form a fairly stiff batter.

3 Grease a heavy frying pan (skillet) or griddle (grill) pan with a little butter and set over a medium-high heat. When it's really hot, add a few large tablespoons of the sweet potato batter. Cook for 3–4 minutes each side until golden brown. Remove and keep warm while you cook the remaining pancakes in the same way.

4 Serve the hot pancakes and crispy bacon with a grinding of black pepper, drizzled with hot sauce.

OR YOU CAN TRY THIS...
– Use soya or almond milk instead of dairy.
– Cook the pancakes in coconut oil rather than butter.
– Serve with fried plantains.

BREAKFAST BURRITOS

SERVES: 4 | **PREP:** 15 MINUTES | **COOK:** 10 MINUTES

8 thin rashers (slices) bacon
4 flour tortillas
6 medium free-range eggs
6 tbsp milk
85g/3oz (scant ¾ cup)
    grated Cheddar cheese
good pinch of crushed dried
    chilli flakes
few sprigs of coriander
    (cilantro), chopped
15g/½oz (1 tbsp) butter
4 heaped tbsp fresh tomato
    salsa
salt and freshly ground
    black pepper
Mexican hot sauce, for
    drizzling

**These spicy egg and bacon burritos are quick and easy to make.
If you like them crispy, you can toast them in a hot frying pan (skillet)
for a few seconds after folding and rolling them.**

1 Cook the bacon in a dry frying pan (skillet) or under a hot grill
(broiler) until it's golden brown and crisp. Remove and drain on
kitchen paper (paper towels).

2 Add the tortillas to the hot frying pan and heat in the bacon fat
over a low-medium heat for a few seconds. Remove and keep warm.

3 In a bowl, whisk the eggs and milk together, then beat in the cheese,
chilli flakes and coriander. Season lightly with salt and pepper.

4 Melt the butter in a non-stick saucepan set over a low heat. Add the
beaten egg mixture and stir with a wooden spoon until the eggs
scramble and set, drawing the mixture in from the sides to the
middle. As soon as they start to set, remove the pan from the heat.

5 Put a warm tortilla on each serving plate and smear with the
tomato salsa. Crumble the crispy bacon over the top and add
the scrambled eggs.

6 Fold the sides of each tortilla over the filling and then roll it up from
the other side. Serve immediately drizzled with Mexican hot sauce.

OR YOU CAN TRY THIS...

– Add some grilled (broiled) or canned red or jalapeño peppers to
the burritos before folding and rolling.
– Add some guacamole or sour cream.
– Add diced spring onions (scallions) to the scrambled egg mixture.
– Add some fresh baby spinach leaves or rocket (arugula).
– Omit the bacon and add some drained canned black beans or
refried beans.

PERUVIAN BRUNCH WITH AJI HOT SAUCE

SERVES: 4 | **PREP:** 10 MINUTES | **COOK:** 20 MINUTES

150g/5oz (scant 1 cup) quinoa (dried weight)

360ml/12fl oz (1½ cups) vegetable or chicken stock

½ tsp cumin seeds

½ tsp fennel seeds

5 tbsp olive oil

1 bunch of coriander (cilantro), chopped

1 ripe avocado, stoned (pitted), peeled and diced

juice of 1 lime

200g/7oz cherry or baby plum tomatoes

1 bunch of spring onions (scallions)

1 x 400g/14oz can (2 cups) kidney beans, rinsed and drained

4 medium free-range eggs

sea salt and freshly ground black pepper

aji hot sauce, for drizzling

TIP: If you're in a hurry, microwave a pouch of ready-to-eat quinoa – it takes seconds!

You can now buy spicy aji (hot chilli pepper) sauces from Peru, Ecuador and Colombia online and in specialist delis. This brunch of quinoa, seeds, griddled vegetables and eggs is a really healthy way to start the day.

1 Rinse the quinoa under running cold water, then drain. Heat the stock in a saucepan and when it starts to boil, add the quinoa. Reduce the heat, cover the pan and simmer gently for about 15 minutes until tender and most of the liquid has been absorbed. When the quinoa is cooked, the 'sprout' or 'tail' will pop out of the seed.

2 Turn off the heat and leave the quinoa to steam in the pan for 5–8 minutes before draining off any excess liquid. Fluff it up with a fork.

3 Meanwhile, toast the seeds in a small dry frying pan (skillet) set over a medium-high heat, shaking the pan occasionally, for 1–2 minutes until fragrant. Remove from the pan.

4 Add 2 tablespoons olive oil, the coriander, avocado and lime juice to the quinoa and mix gently together. Season to taste with salt and pepper.

5 Heat 1 tablespoon oil in a griddle (grill) pan and cook the tomatoes and whole spring onions over a medium-high heat until just tender and starting to char. Add the beans and warm through quickly.

6 Fry the eggs in the remaining olive oil until the whites are set and crisp and golden brown around the edges.

7 Divide the quinoa between 4 plates and top with a fried egg. Serve with the vegetables and black beans, drizzled with aji hot sauce.

OR YOU CAN TRY THIS...

– Drizzle the brunch with West Indian hot sauce or add a few shakes of Tabasco.
– Add some diced chorizo or crumbled crispy bacon.

LIGHT
LUNCHES

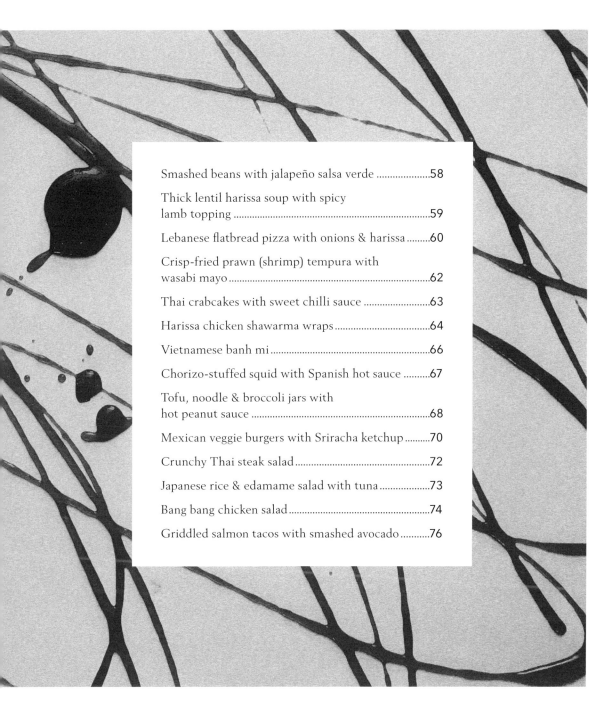

SMASHED BEANS WITH JALAPEÑO SALSA VERDE

SERVES: 4 | **PREP:** 15 MINUTES | **COOK:** 20 MINUTES

4 red, green or yellow
   (bell) peppers, deseeded
   and cut into chunks
2 aubergines (eggplants),
   cubed
5 tbsp olive oil
2 x 400g/14oz cans
   (4 cups) butter beans
   (lima beans), rinsed
   and drained
2 garlic cloves, crushed
grated zest and juice of
   1 juicy lemon
½ tsp cumin seeds
½ tsp coriander seeds
sea salt and freshly ground
   black pepper

Jalapeño salsa verde:
2 jalapeño chillies, chopped
1 large garlic clove, crushed
2 spring onions (scallions),
   chopped
1 large bunch of coriander
   (cilantro), stems and
   leaves chopped
juice of 1 lime
3 tbsp olive oil
1 tbsp red wine vinegar
good pinch of brown sugar
pinch of sea salt crystals

This easy meal is very versatile – you can serve the smashed beans with meat and fish dishes or top them with roasted vegetables (see below). The salsa verde is a staple Mexican sauce; for a more authentic version add some canned or fresh tomatillos. If you don't have the time or ingredients to make the sauce yourself, drizzle the beans and vegetables with some bottled Mexican or West Indian hot sauce.

1 Preheat the oven to 200°C, 400°F, gas mark 6.

2 Arrange the peppers and aubergines in a large roasting pan and drizzle with 3 tablespoons of the olive oil. Grind over a little salt and pepper. Roast in the preheated oven for about 20 minutes until tender and starting to char.

3 Make the jalapeño salsa verde: put all the ingredients in a blender and blitz until you have a smooth green paste. Transfer to a bowl.

4 Meanwhile, put the beans in a large bowl with the remaining olive oil, garlic, lemon zest and juice and mash them coarsely. Season to taste with salt and pepper.

5 Toast the seeds in a small dry frying pan (skillet) for 1–2 minutes until they release their aroma and start to colour. Remove immediately and add to the smashed beans.

6 Divide the beans between 4 serving plates and top with the roasted vegetables. Drizzle the jalapeño salsa verde over the top.

OR YOU CAN TRY THIS...
– Instead of butter beans (lima beans), use canned cannellini, haricot or flageolet beans.
– Add some capers or cornichons (tiny gherkins) to the salsa verde.
– Top the smashed beans with griddled chicken or prawns (shrimp).

THICK LENTIL HARISSA SOUP WITH SPICY LAMB TOPPING

SERVES: 4 | **PREP:** 10 MINUTES | **COOK:** 35–40 MINUTES

3 tbsp olive oil
1 large onion, finely chopped
2 large carrots, diced
3 garlic cloves, crushed
2.5cm/1in piece fresh
    root ginger, peeled and
    chopped
2 tsp black mustard seeds
½ tsp cumin seeds
1 tsp ground turmeric
1 tsp ground cinnamon
300g/10oz fresh tomatoes,
    skinned and chopped
250g/9oz (1¼ cups) split
    red lentils (dry weight)
1.2 litres/2 pints (5 cups)
    vegetable or chicken stock
1 tbsp harissa
4 tbsp 0%-fat Greek yoghurt
handful of coriander
    (cilantro), chopped
sea salt and freshly ground
    black pepper

Spicy lamb:
2 tbsp olive oil
1 onion, diced
1 red chilli, diced
1 tsp paprika
300g/10oz (scant 1½ cups)
    minced (ground) lamb
2 tbsp tomato purée (paste)
pinch of sugar
240ml/8fl oz (1 cup) water

Make the lentil soup in advance and store it in the fridge for 3–4 days or freeze it until required. Cook the spicy lamb just before serving.

1 Make the soup: heat the oil in a large saucepan over a low-medium heat and cook the onion, carrots, garlic and ginger, stirring occasionally, for 6–8 minutes until softened. Add the mustard and cumin seeds and cook for 2 minutes. Stir in the ground spices, tomatoes and lentils and cook for 1 minute.

2 Add the stock and bring to the boil. Reduce the heat and simmer gently for 25–30 minutes until the lentils are cooked and mushy and the soup has thickened. Stir in the harissa and season with salt and pepper to taste.

3 Meanwhile, make the spicy lamb: Heat the olive oil in another pan over a medium heat and cook the onion and chilli for 6–8 minutes, stirring occasionally, until tender. Stir in the paprika and lamb and cook for 3–4 minutes until the lamb is browned all over. Add the remaining ingredients and cook for 5–10 minutes until the liquid reduces and evaporates. Season to taste.

4 Ladle the soup into 4 shallow serving bowls and swirl in a spoonful of yoghurt. Top with the spicy lamb and serve sprinkled with the chopped coriander.

OR YOU CAN TRY THIS...

– Add a few strands of saffron with the stock.
– Add some baby spinach leaves to the spicy lamb.
– Vegetarians can top the soup with some crisp fried onions and chickpeas instead of lamb.
– Add some finely chopped preserved lemon or sprinkle with lemon juice.

LEBANESE FLATBREAD PIZZA WITH ONIONS & HARISSA

SERVES: 4 | **PREP:** 10 MINUTES | **COOK:** 30 MINUTES

2 tbsp olive oil, plus extra
    for greasing
2 large onions, finely sliced
few drops of balsamic
    vinegar
1 tsp sugar
400g/14oz spinach,
    shredded
4 x 20cm/8in flatbreads
3 juicy plum tomatoes,
    quartered
125g/4oz feta cheese, diced
12–16 black olives, stoned
    (pitted)
4 tbsp pine nuts
½–1 tsp harissa paste
100g/3½oz (scant ½ cup)
    0%-fat Greek yoghurt
few sprigs of mint, finely
    chopped
sea salt crystals

1 Preheat the oven to 200°C, 400°F, gas mark 6.

2 Heat the olive oil in a large frying pan (skillet) set over a medium heat. Add the onions and cook, stirring occasionally, for 10 minutes or until tender and golden brown. Add the balsamic vinegar and sugar and cook for 3–4 minutes. Season to taste with salt.

3 Meanwhile, cook the spinach with 1 tablespoon water in a large covered saucepan over a medium heat for about 2 minutes, shaking occasionally, until the leaves wilt and turn bright green. Drain well in a colander, pressing down with a saucer to extract all the liquid, and keep warm.

4 Heat the flatbreads on an oiled griddle (grill) pan for 3–4 minutes each side. Remove and place them on baking trays (cookie sheets). Spread the spinach and cooked onions on top of the flatbreads. Add the tomatoes, feta and olives. Sprinkle the pine nuts over the top.

5 Cook in the preheated oven for 5–7 minutes until hot and crisp, the tomatoes are tender and the pine nuts are golden brown.

6 Meanwhile, swirl the harissa into the yoghurt.

7 Serve the pizzas topped with a spoonful or two of harissa yoghurt and sprinkled with mint.

OR YOU CAN TRY THIS...
– Scatter some pomegranate seeds over the top before serving.
– Smear the flatbread with some tomato purée (paste) or red pesto before adding the onions.
– Cook some garlic with the onions.
– Add some seeds (fennel, cumin, caraway, sesame) to the onions while they're cooking.
– Sprinkle with za'atar or paprika to finish.

CRISP-FRIED PRAWN (SHRIMP) TEMPURA WITH WASABI MAYO

SERVES: 4 | **PREP:** 15 MINUTES | **COOK:** 10–12 MINUTES

1 medium free-range egg

240ml/8fl oz (1 cup) ice-cold water

100g/3½oz (generous ¾ cup) plain (all-purpose) flour

30g/1oz (¼ cup) cornflour (cornstarch)

½ tsp salt

oil, for deep-frying

500g/1lb 2oz shelled raw king prawns (jumbo shrimp)

120ml/4fl oz (½ cup) light mayonnaise

2 tsp wasabi

1 red chilli, finely sliced

Lemon salsa:

1 preserved lemon, pulp discarded and skin diced

2 juicy tomatoes, deseeded and diced

1 small bunch of flat-leaf parsley, chopped

handful of chives, snipped

2 tbsp olive oil

Wasabi is a type of Japanese horseradish, which is extremely hot. We've mixed it into some mayonnaise to make a hot sauce to accompany the tempura.

1 First make the tempura batter: in a large mixing bowl, beat the egg and stir in the water. Gently beat in the flour, cornflour and salt – don't over-whisk as you need a few lumps. Set aside.

2 Make the preserved lemon salsa: stir all the ingredients together in a bowl.

3 Heat the oil in a deep heavy-based saucepan or deep-fryer until it reaches 180°C/350°F. You can use a thermometer to check the temperature. If you don't have one, add a cube of bread – the oil is ready when the bread cube sizzles and turns brown in 25 seconds.

4 Dip the prawns into the batter and then fry in batches, a few at a time, for 2–3 minutes until crisp and golden. Remove with a slotted spoon and drain on kitchen paper (paper towels).

5 Stir the mayonnaise and wasabi together in a bowl.

6 Divide the prawns between 4 serving plates and scatter the sliced chilli over the top. Serve immediately with the lemon salsa and wasabi mayo.

OR YOU CAN TRY THIS...

– Instead of prawns, use squid or vegetables such as aubergines (eggplants), asparagus, green beans, courgettes (zucchini), button mushrooms and broccoli or cauliflower florets.

– For a more substantial meal, serve the tempura with some plain boiled rice.

THAI CRABCAKES WITH SWEET CHILLI SAUCE

SERVES: 4 | **PREP:** 25 MINUTES | **CHILL:** 15–30 MINUTES | **COOK:** 4–6 MINUTES/BATCH

500g/1lb 2oz fresh white
   crabmeat
60g/2oz breadcrumbs
2 red bird's eye chillies, diced
4 spring onions (scallions),
   sliced
2 garlic cloves, crushed
1 stalk lemongrass, peeled
   and chopped
4 fresh kaffir lime leaves,
   finely shredded
small bunch of coriander
   (cilantro), stems and leaves
2 tsp nam pla (Thai fish sauce)
2 tbsp light mayonnaise
flour, for dusting
groundnut (peanut) or
   sunflower oil, for frying
sweet chilli sauce, for dipping

Crunchy salad:
200g/7oz bean sprouts
2 carrots, peeled and cut
   into matchsticks
1 red, yellow or green (bell)
   pepper, diced
6 spring onions (scallions),
   sliced
8 crisp radishes, thinly sliced
1 red chilli, cut into strips
2 tbsp nam pla (Thai fish
   sauce)
juice of 1 lime
pinch of sugar

These spicy little crabcakes make a great light lunch. Alternatively, make them smaller, dividing the mixture into 24 bite-sized balls, and serve at parties or with pre-dinner drinks. For best results use fresh crabmeat, but if it's not available frozen or canned is fine.

1 Put the crabmeat, breadcrumbs, chillies, spring onions, garlic, lemongrass, lime leaves, coriander, nam pla and mayonnaise in a blender or food processor and blitz until you have a thick paste.

2 Divide the mixture into 12 portions and shape with your hands into little patties. Dust lightly with flour and chill in the fridge for 15–30 minutes to firm them up.

3 Meanwhile, make the crunchy salad: mix together the bean sprouts, carrots, pepper, spring onions and radishes. Blend the chilli, nam pla and lime juice in a smaller bowl and sweeten to taste. Pour over the salad and toss gently.

4 Heat the oil in a large frying pan (skillet) over a medium-high heat. Fry the crabcakes in batches for 2–3 minutes each side until crisp and golden brown. Take care when you turn them over – use a spatula and do it gently to keep their shape. Remove and keep warm while you fry the rest.

5 Serve the hot crabcakes with the crunchy salad and small individual dishes of sweet chilli sauce for dipping.

OR YOU CAN TRY THIS...
– Add some cucumber, shredded Chinese leaves or cabbage to the salad.
– Use green chillies instead of red.
– Substitute soy sauce for the nam pla.
– Add a teaspoon of grated root ginger to the crabcakes.

HARISSA CHICKEN SHAWARMA WRAPS

SERVES: 4 | **PREP:** 15 MINUTES | **MARINATE:** AT LEAST 1 HOUR | **COOK:** 10–15 MINUTES

4 chicken breasts, skinless
and boneless
1 tsp fennel seeds
240g/8½oz (1 cup)
0%-fat Greek yoghurt
few sprigs of fennel leaves,
finely chopped
squeeze of lemon juice
1–2 tsp harissa paste
4 stems of cherry tomatoes
on the vine
4 large pitta breads
pickled cucumbers or
hot chillies, to serve

Shawarma marinade:
125g/4oz (½ cup) 0%-fat
Greek yoghurt
juice of 1 lemon
3 garlic cloves, crushed
1 tsp grated fresh root
ginger
1 tsp ground cumin
1 tsp paprika
pinch of ground nutmeg
¼ tsp dried oregano or thyme
good pinch of salt

Spicy, aromatic chicken shawarma is popular throughout the Middle East. It's usually served in pitta bread with pickled cucumber and pungent garlic sauce but we've used fennel-flavoured yoghurt with a dash of fiery red harissa instead.

1 Mix all the ingredients for the marinade in a shallow dish.

2 Cut each chicken breast in half horizontally so you end up with 2 thin escalopes (or bash with a rolling pin between 2 sheets of baking parchment (parchment paper) to flatten them out). Add to the marinade and coat the chicken all over. Cover the dish and leave in the fridge for at least 1 hour (overnight, if wished).

3 Meanwhile, heat a small frying pan (skillet) over a high heat. Add the fennel seeds and cook for about 1 minute, tossing them occasionally, until golden brown and they release their aroma. Take care that they don't burn. Remove from the pan immediately and stir into the yoghurt with the chopped fennel leaves and lemon juice. Swirl in the harissa.

4 Set a griddle (grill) pan over a high heat and when it's really hot, add the marinated chicken. Cook for 4–5 minutes each side until golden brown and thoroughly cooked inside. Remove from the pan and griddle the tomatoes until they are just tender and starting to char.

5 Warm the pitta breads in a griddle (grill) pan or in a low oven and cut them open down one side with a sharp knife.

6 Cut the chicken into really thin slices and divide between the split pitta breads, stuffing it into the middle with the pickled cucumbers or chillies. Add a spoonful of fennel and harissa yoghurt and serve with the griddled tomatoes.

OR YOU CAN TRY THIS...
– Add some diced feta or a little tahini.
– Use hummus instead of fennel yoghurt.

VIETNAMESE BANH MI

SERVES: 4 | **PREP:** 20 MINUTES | **STAND:** AT LEAST 1 HOUR | **COOK:** 10 MINUTES

2 carrots, cut into thin
    matchsticks
4 radishes, thinly sliced
1 red (bell) pepper, deseeded
    and thinly sliced
1 small ridged cucumber,
    thinly sliced
4 tbsp rice vinegar
4 tbsp caster (superfine)
    sugar
1 tbsp nam pla (Thai fish
    sauce)
4 small baguettes (French
    sticks), halved and
    hollowed out
1 red onion, thinly sliced

Sriracha mayo:
120g/4oz (½ cup)
    mayonnaise
2 spring onions (scallions),
    diced
2 tbsp Sriracha
sea salt crystals

Spicy beef:
1 tbsp olive oil
300g/10oz (scant 1½ cups)
    minced (ground) lean
    beef (less than 5% fat)
3 garlic cloves, crushed
1 red bird's eye chilli, diced
handful of coriander
    (cilantro), chopped

The most delicious sandwich of all time, this takes longer to make than most but is well worth the extra effort. We have used Sriracha but you can substitute your favourite hot sauce – sweet Thai chilli sauce works really well.

1 Make the Sriracha mayo: mix all the ingredients together, seasoning to taste with salt. Cover and leave in the fridge until you're ready to assemble the baguettes.

2 Mix together the carrots, radishes, red pepper and cucumber in a glass bowl. Heat the vinegar and sugar in a small pan, stirring until the sugar dissolves, then bring to the boil and remove from the heat. Stir in the nam pla and pour over the vegetables. Set aside for at least 1 hour – the longer the better.

3 Just before you're ready to eat, make the spicy beef: heat the oil in a frying pan (skillet) set over a medium-high heat. Add the beef and cook, stirring, until browned all over. Stir in the garlic and chilli and cook for 2–3 minutes. Stir in the coriander.

4 Split the baguettes in half lengthwise and scoop out some of the soft bread in the centre to leave a crusty shell.

5 Spread the Sriracha mayo over the bases and then add the minced beef mixture. Top with the carrot and radish mixture and the sliced red onion. Cover with the baguette tops, pressing down firmly.

6 Eat immediately while the spicy beef is still warm. Drizzle with some more Sriracha, if wished.

OR YOU CAN TRY THIS...
– Use sliced Japanese daikon instead of radishes.
– Add some pickled chillies to the baguette.
– Try chopped Thai basil or mint instead of coriander (cilantro).

CHORIZO-STUFFED SQUID WITH SPANISH HOT SAUCE

SERVES: 4 | **PREP:** 15 MINUTES | **COOK:** 35–45 MINUTES

450g/1lb baby plum tomatoes, halved
2 large red (bell) peppers, deseeded and sliced
60ml/2fl oz (4 tbsp) olive oil
1 onion, chopped
2 garlic cloves, crushed
1 tsp paprika
200g/7oz chorizo, skinned and diced
1 small bunch of flat-leaf parsley, finely chopped
500g/1lb 2oz prepared squid (see note below)
sea salt and freshly ground black pepper
piri piri sauce, for drizzling
toasted crusty bread, to serve

PREPARING SQUID:
1 Pull out the tentacles from inside the squid tube.
2 Cut off the fins.
3 Peel off and discard any loose skin.
4 Rinse everything under cold running water and pat dry with kitchen paper (paper towels).
5 Cut the tentacles into small pieces.

This dish is an unusual variant on the surf and turf theme, and it tastes equally good served hot or cold. If you're squeamish about preparing the squid, ask your fishmonger to do it for you. You want to end up with whole tubes ready to stuff, and separate tentacles and fins, which are chopped into small pieces.

1 Preheat the oven to 190°C, 375°F, gas mark 5.

2 Arrange the plum tomatoes and red peppers in a roasting tin (pan) and sprinkle 2 tablespoons of the olive oil over them. Season lightly with salt and pepper. Roast in the preheated oven for 20–25 minutes until tender.

3 Meanwhile, heat 1 tablespoon olive oil in a frying pan (skillet) over a low-medium heat. Cook the onion and garlic, stirring occasionally, until tender and golden. Stir in the paprika and cook for 1 minute.

4 Add the chorizo, most of the parsley (reserving some for the garnish) and the chopped squid tentacles and fins. Cook for 5 minutes, stirring occasionally, and season.

5 Spoon the chorizo mixture into the hollow squid tubes and score each one 2–3 times with a sharp knife. Place, scored-side up, on top of the roasted tomatoes and peppers and drizzle over the rest of the oil.

6 Bake in the oven for 15–20 minutes until the squid is cooked and tender. Serve sprinkled with the remaining parsley and drizzled with piri piri sauce, with some toasted bread on the side.

OR YOU CAN TRY THIS...
– You can use canned chopped tomatoes and mix them with the roasted peppers before cooking the squid.
– Drizzle with any hot sauce of your choice, e.g. Sriracha or Tabasco.
– For more heat, add a diced chilli to the chorizo mixture.

TOFU, NOODLE & BROCCOLI JARS WITH HOT PEANUT SAUCE

SERVES: 4 | **PREP:** 10 MINUTES | **COOK:** 10 MINUTES | **STAND:** 5 MINUTES

480ml/16fl oz (2 cups) vegetable stock
2 tbsp soy sauce or tamari
1 red chilli, deseeded and diced
2.5cm/1in piece fresh root ginger, peeled and diced
2 garlic cloves, crushed
300g/10oz small broccoli florets
150g/5oz fresh thin egg noodles
250g/9oz tofu, cubed

Hot peanut sauce:
2 tbsp groundnut (peanut) or vegetable oil
125g/4oz (½ cup) crunchy peanut butter
1–2 tbsp Sriracha
few drops of soy sauce or tamari

This is a healthy noodle and vegetable soup in a glass jar – the wide Mason ones work very well. Of course, you can ladle it into shallow bowls instead if you prefer.

1 Put the vegetable stock, soy sauce (or tamari), chilli, ginger and garlic in a large saucepan and bring to the boil.

2 Add the broccoli and cook for 2–3 minutes. Add the noodles and boil for 1–2 minutes until tender and al dente.

3 Stir in the tofu and remove the pan from the heat. Cover and set aside for 5 minutes.

4 Meanwhile, make the hot peanut sauce: put all the ingredients in a food processor or food chopper and blitz to a coarse purée.

5 Divide the tofu, noodle and broccoli mixture between 4 wide-mouthed glass jars and top with the hot peanut sauce.

OR YOU CAN TRY THIS...
– Use Japanese soba noodles and cook them separately according to the packet instructions before adding to the broccoli mixture.
– If you don't eat peanuts, top with some sweet chilli sauce.
– Use smoked tofu instead of plain.
– Add some more vegetables, e.g. baby asparagus or chopped fine green beans.
– For a Japanese touch, add some miso paste to the hot stock.

MEXICAN VEGGIE BURGERS WITH SRIRACHA KETCHUP

SERVES: 4 | **PREP:** 15 MINUTES | **CHILL:** 1 HOUR | **COOK:** 20 MINUTES

1 tbsp olive oil, plus extra
for shallow-frying
1 red onion, finely chopped
3 garlic cloves, crushed
1 jalapeño chilli, deseeded
and diced
½ tsp ground cumin
2 x 400g/14oz cans
(scant 5 cups) chickpeas,
rinsed and drained
few sprigs of coriander
(cilantro), chopped
juice of ½ lime
1 medium free-range egg,
beaten
60g/2oz (generous 1 cup)
fresh breadcrumbs
4 burger buns, split and
toasted
crisp lettuce leaves,
e.g. cos (romaine)
guacamole, to serve
sea salt and freshly ground
black pepper

Sriracha ketchup:
120ml/4fl oz (½ cup)
tomato ketchup
2 tbsp Sriracha
juice of ½ lime
1 tsp rice vinegar
1 tsp clear honey

These spicy veggie burgers are very filling and are great for brunch, a light lunch or a TV dinner. If you don't want to bother making the Sriracha ketchup you can now buy it ready bottled in some supermarkets, although it won't taste quite so good.

1 Heat the olive oil in a frying pan (skillet) over a low-medium heat and cook the onion and garlic for 6–8 minutes until softened. Stir in the chilli and cumin and cook for 2 minutes.

2 Coarsely mash the chickpeas in a large bowl and stir in the cooked onion mixture. Allow to cool for a few minutes and then stir in the coriander, lime juice, beaten egg and breadcrumbs and season.

3 Divide the mixture into 4 portions and shape each one into a burger. Cover and chill in the fridge for 1 hour to firm them up.

4 Meanwhile, make the Sriracha ketchup: mix all the ingredients together in a bowl, stirring well.

5 Heat a little olive oil in a non-stick frying pan (skillet) set over a medium heat. Add the burgers to the hot pan and cook for 4–5 minutes each side until crisp and golden brown. Turn them over and remove them carefully.

6 Put them in toasted burger buns with some crisp lettuce, guacamole and the Sriracha ketchup. Serve immediately.

OR YOU CAN TRY THIS...

– Use red kidney beans or black beans instead of chickpeas, or a mixture of all three.
– Top the burgers with a spoonful of Sriracha mayo.
– Cover each burger with a slice of cheese (Monterey Jack, Emmenthal or Cheddar) and melt under a hot grill (broiler).

CRUNCHY THAI STEAK SALAD

SERVES: 4 | **PREP:** 15 MINUTES | **COOK:** 3–6 MINUTES

1 red (bell) pepper, deseeded
and thinly sliced
1 large carrot, cut into thin
matchsticks
½ cucumber, cut into thin
matchsticks
1 bunch of spring onions
(scallions), thinly sliced
large handful of bean sprouts
1 mango, peeled, stoned
(pitted) and cut into
matchsticks
handful of coriander
(cilantro), chopped
4 sirloin steaks
oil, for brushing
small bunch of Thai basil or
mint, chopped
1 red chilli, shredded
30g/1oz (¼ cup) roasted
peanuts, chopped
lime wedges, for serving

Sriracha dressing:
3 tbsp groundnut (peanut) oil
1 tsp toasted sesame oil
2 tbsp nam pla (Thai fish
sauce)
1 tbsp soy sauce
1 tsp Sriracha
1 tbsp rice vinegar
juice of 1 lime
1 garlic clove, crushed
1 tsp sugar

This crunchy salad is not only healthy but also very refreshing. It's best eaten while the steak is still warm. To make it more substantial, serve with some boiled rice or noodles.

1 Make the Sriracha dressing: put all the ingredients in a bowl and whisk together until thoroughly combined.

2 Put the red pepper, carrot, cucumber, spring onions, bean sprouts, mango and coriander in a large bowl and mix together gently.

3 Season the steaks with salt and pepper and brush lightly with oil. Grill (broil) them on a ridged griddle (grill) pan set over a medium-high heat for about 2–3 minutes each side until browned and attractively striped on the outside but still pink on the inside (cook for 5–6 minutes if you like your steak well done). Remove and cut into thin strips.

4 Add the steak to the salad and toss in the Sriracha dressing. Divide between 4 serving plates and sprinkle the herbs, chilli and peanuts over the top. Serve immediately while the steak is still warm, with lime wedges alongside.

OR YOU CAN TRY THIS...

– Instead of steak, grill (broil) some chicken breasts or salmon fillets.
– Vegetarians can add some crunchy beans to the salad. Try a mixture of steamed fine green beans and edamame.
– Use sweet chilli sauce instead of Sriracha in the dressing.
– Add some crunchy peanut butter to the dressing.

JAPANESE RICE & EDAMAME SALAD WITH TUNA

SERVES: 4 | **PREP:** 15 MINUTES | **COOK:** 20 MINUTES

225g/8oz (1 cup) brown rice (dry weight)
125g/4oz (generous 1½ cups) frozen edamame beans
2 carrots, diced
150g/5oz (2¼ cups) sprouted seeds, e.g. mizuna, mung, radish
4 spring onions (scallions), sliced diagonally
few sprigs of coriander (cilantro), chopped
olive oil, for brushing
4 x 100g/3½oz tuna steaks
1 sheet ready-toasted sushi nori, cut into thin shreds
2 tbsp toasted black or white sesame seeds

Wasabi dressing:
1 tbsp sunflower oil
1 tbsp toasted sesame oil
1 tsp wasabi paste
1 tbsp rice vinegar
1 tsp soy sauce
juice of ½ lime
1 garlic clove, crushed
2 tsp grated fresh root ginger
2 tsp honey

The hot wasabi dressing gives this salad its distinctive flavour. When making the dressing, taste it to get the right balance between the heat of the wasabi and the sweetness of the honey.

1 Cook the brown rice according to the instructions on the packet. Set aside to cool in a large bowl.

2 Cook the beans in a pan of boiling water for 3 minutes. Refresh under running cold water, then drain and set aside.

3 Make the wasabi dressing: whisk all the ingredients together until well blended. Alternatively, place them in a screwtop jar and shake vigorously.

4 Gently stir the rice with a fork to break up any clumps and separate the grains. Mix in the beans, carrots, sprouted seeds, spring onions and coriander. Pour most of the dressing over the top and toss gently together.

5 Lightly brush a non-stick griddle (grill) pan with oil and place over a medium-high heat. Add the tuna steaks and cook for 2–3 minutes each side, depending on how well cooked you like them. Cut into slices.

6 Divide the rice salad between 4 serving plates. Top each one with sliced tuna and drizzle with the remaining dressing. Sprinkle with the shredded nori and sesame seeds.

OR YOU CAN TRY THIS...

– Instead of tuna use sliced griddled (grilled) chicken or tofu.
– Add some avocado, radishes, red or yellow (bell) peppers, cooked soya beans or chopped coriander (cilantro) to the rice salad.
– Use wild or black rice instead of brown.

BANG BANG CHICKEN SALAD

SERVES: 4 | **PREP:** 15 MINUTES | **COOK:** 4–5 MINUTES

200g/7oz rice noodles
(dried weight)
150g/5oz bean sprouts
1 large carrot, cut into strips
with a vegetable peeler
4 spring onions (scallions),
shredded
1 small bunch of coriander
(cilantro), chopped
400g/14oz cooked chicken
breasts, skinned and
shredded
1 tbsp sesame seeds
50g/2oz roasted peanuts,
coarsely chopped

Spicy peanut dressing:
2 tbsp peanut butter
1 tbsp groundnut (peanut)
oil
2.5cm/1in piece fresh root
ginger, peeled and diced
1 tbsp toasted sesame oil
1 tbsp soy sauce
1 tbsp Sriracha or sweet
chilli sauce
1 tbsp rice wine vinegar
juice of 1 lime
1 tsp honey

This quick and easy salad is a great way to use up leftover roast or poached chicken or turkey. Vegetarians can enjoy this by substituting edamame beans or chickpeas – use canned or frozen for convenience.

1 Cook the noodles according to the instructions on the packet. Drain well.

2 Put the bean sprouts, carrot, spring onions, coriander and chicken in a large bowl.

3 Make the spicy peanut dressing: blitz all the ingredients in a blender until smooth.

4 Toast the sesame seeds in a small dry frying pan (skillet) over a medium-high heat. Cook for 1–2 minutes, shaking gently, until they turn golden and fragrant. Take care that they don't burn. Remove from the pan.

5 Mix the rice noodles into the chicken salad and toss gently in the spicy peanut dressing.

6 Divide between 4 serving plates and sprinkle with the chopped peanuts and toasted sesame seeds.

OR YOU CAN TRY THIS...

– Poach or grill (broil) some chicken breasts, cut into thin slices and add to the salad vegetables and noodles.
– For a lighter salad, omit the rice noodles.
– Add some sliced mango, papaya or pink grapefruit.
– Use maple syrup instead of honey.
– Substitute turkey for the chicken.
– Add finely sliced red or green (bell) peppers, courgette (zucchini) matchsticks and shredded greens.

GRIDDLED SALMON TACOS WITH SMASHED AVOCADO

SERVES: 4 | **PREP:** 15 MINUTES | **COOK:** 5 MINUTES

4 x 100g/3½oz salmon
    fillets, skinned and boned
1 tsp paprika
1 x 400g/14oz can black
    beans, rinsed and drained
4 spring onions (scallions),
    chopped
8 cherry or baby plum
    tomatoes, chopped
1 red chilli, deseeded and
    diced
handful of coriander
    (cilantro), chopped
juice of 1 lime
8 small corn tortillas
sea salt and freshly ground
    black pepper
Mexican hot sauce, for
    drizzling

Smashed avocado:
2 ripe avocados, stoned
    (pitted) and peeled
few drops of Tabasco
handful of coriander
    (cilantro), chopped
juice of ½ lime

Everyone loves tacos and this is a good way to get children eating some of their 5-a-day vegetables and nutritious omega-3 fish oils. Healthy and colourful, it's a great dish for when you're in a hurry.

1 Sprinkle the salmon fillets with the paprika and season with salt and pepper. Cook under a hot grill (broiler) or in a hot griddle (grill) pan for about 5 minutes until slightly browned and cooked right through. Cut into chunks.

2 Meanwhile, mix the black beans, spring onions, tomatoes, chilli, coriander and lime juice in a bowl. Season to taste with salt and pepper.

3 Make the smashed avocado: mash the avocado flesh roughly with a fork and stir in the Tabasco, coriander and lime juice. Add a little salt to taste.

4 Warm the tortillas and divide the black bean salsa mixture and salmon between them. Top with the smashed avocado and serve drizzled with hot sauce.

OR YOU CAN TRY THIS...

– Use griddled (grilled) prawns (shrimp) or chicken instead of salmon.
– Substitute red kidney beans for the black beans.
– Add some quinoa or freekeh for a more substantial dish.
– Sprinkle the tacos with freshly squeezed lime juice.
– Instead of smashed avocado, top with a large spoonful of guacamole.
– Use canned salmon or tuna.

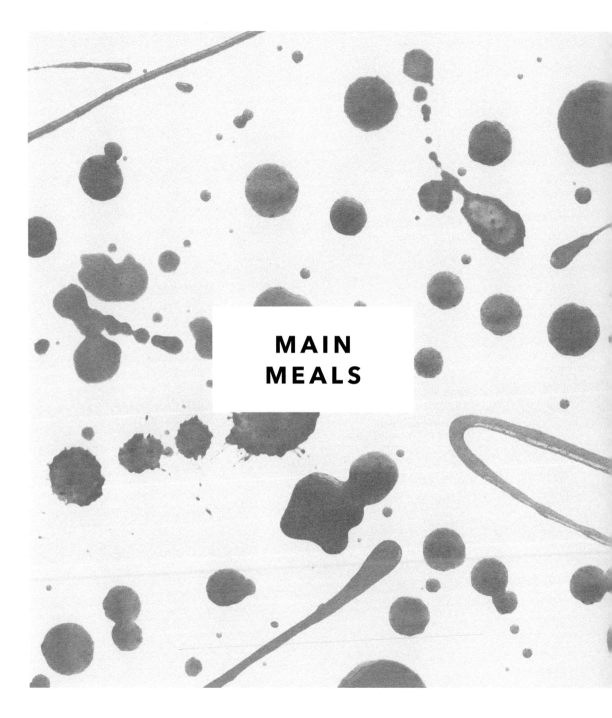

MAIN
MEALS

JAMAICAN JERK CHICKEN WITH RICE & PEAS

SERVES: 4 | **PREP:** 20 MINUTES | **MARINATE:** AT LEAST 1 HOUR | **COOK:** 30 MINUTES

8 chicken thighs, skin on, bone in
350g/12oz (1½ cups) long-grain rice (dry weight)
400ml/14fl oz (generous 1½ cups) canned coconut milk
360ml/12fl oz (1½ cups) water
2 garlic cloves, crushed
½ tsp salt
1 x 400g/14oz can (2 cups) kidney beans, rinsed and drained
small handful of coriander (cilantro), chopped
West Indian hot sauce, for drizzling

Don't be put off by the long list of ingredients for the jerk seasoning. You can use the ready-ground powder you buy in little pots in supermarkets if you prefer, but it lacks the heat, spice and intensity of flavour of the freshly made marinade. Rice and 'peas' is a staple in Jamaica and is on nearly every menu. The 'peas' are actually beans – usually red kidney beans but sometimes black beans.

1 Make the jerk seasoning: crush the allspice and peppercorns with a pestle and mortar. Put them in a blender with the ground spices, thyme, shallot, garlic, ginger, chillies and sugar and blitz to a paste. Transfer to a bowl and stir in the soy sauce, oil, tomato ketchup and lime juice.

2 Using a sharp knife, cut some slits in each chicken thigh. Add them to the jerk seasoning mixture, turning them until well coated all over. Cover and leave in the fridge to marinate for at least 1 hour or, better still, overnight.

3 Preheat the oven to 190°C, 375°F, gas mark 5.

4 Put the chicken thighs in a roasting tin (pan) and spoon over the jerk seasoning marinade. Cook in the preheated oven for about 30 minutes until crisp, well browned and cooked right through.

5 Meanwhile, put the rice in a deep saucepan with the coconut milk, water, garlic and salt. Bring to the boil, then add the canned beans, reduce the heat and cover the pan. Simmer for 15 minutes, stirring occasionally to prevent the rice sticking to the pan, until all the liquid has been absorbed. Leave to stand for 5 minutes, then fluff up with a fork.

6 Serve the jerk chicken with the hot rice, sprinkled with coriander. Drizzle some hot sauce over the top.

Jerk seasoning:
2 tsp allspice berries
2 tsp black peppercorns
good pinch of ground
    nutmeg
good pinch of ground
    cinnamon
4 sprigs of thyme, leaves
    picked
1 shallot, diced
2 garlic cloves, crushed
2.5cm/1in piece fresh root
    ginger, peeled and diced
2 Scotch bonnet or habanero
    chillies, diced
2 tsp brown sugar
1 tbsp soy sauce
1 tbsp olive oil or vegetable
    oil
4 tbsp tomato ketchup
juice of 1 lime

OR YOU CAN TRY THIS...

– Add some clear honey to the jerk seasoning sauce for added sweetness and stickiness.
– Use black beans instead of kidney beans.
– Stir some fresh thyme leaves or a pinch of dried thyme into the rice before cooking.
– Substitute chicken wings or breasts for the thighs.

SPICY GREEK MEATBALLS WITH AVGOLEMONO SAUCE

SERVES: 4 | **PREP:** 15 MINUTES | **CHILL:** 15 MINUTES | **COOK:** 25 MINUTES

2 tbsp olive oil, plus extra
   for frying
1 onion, finely chopped
2 garlic cloves, crushed
500g/1lb 2oz (2¼ cups)
   minced (ground) lamb
½ tsp ground allspice
½ tsp ground coriander
1 small bunch of parsley,
   finely chopped
handful of dill, chopped
60g/2oz (1 cup) fresh
   white breadcrumbs
1 tsp salt
freshly ground black pepper
dash of harissa, plus extra
   to serve
boiled rice, to serve
seeds of ½ pomegranate,
   to serve

Avgolemono sauce:
2 medium free-range eggs
juice of 2 lemons
1 tbsp flour
480ml/16fl oz (2 cups)
   hot chicken stock
sea salt and freshly ground
   black pepper

Meatballs in an egg and lemon sauce are a classic Greek dish. For the best flavour, you must use good-quality chicken stock. If you don't have time to make it yourself, buy it ready-made from a deli or good supermarket.

1 Heat the oil in a large frying pan (skillet) and cook the onion and garlic over a medium heat, stirring occasionally, for 6–8 minutes until softened. Remove from the pan and set aside to cool.

2 In a bowl, mix the cooked onion and garlic with the lamb, ground spices, herbs and breadcrumbs. Add the salt and a little black pepper, then stir in the harissa (not too much as it is very fiery).

3 Divide the mixture into 12 or 16 equal-sized portions and mould into balls with your hands. Cover and chill in the fridge for 15 minutes.

4 Add 1–2 tablespoons oil to the pan in which the onion was fried and set over a medium heat. Fry the meatballs, turning them gently from time to time, for about 10 minutes until cooked and brown.

5 Make the avgolemono sauce: beat the eggs in a bowl and then whisk in the lemon juice and flour until the mixture is smooth and free from lumps. Whisk in a ladle of hot chicken stock followed by another until well combined.

6 Tip the egg and lemon mixture into a pan of simmering hot stock and stir with a wooden spoon over a low-medium heat for about 5 minutes until the sauce has thickened and coats the back of the spoon. Add the meatballs and warm through for a few minutes.

7 Serve the meatballs in the sauce with some boiled rice, sprinkled with pomegranate seeds with some harissa on the side.

OR YOU CAN TRY THIS...
– Use really lean minced (ground) beef (less than 5% fat) instead of lamb.

STICKY ROSE HARISSA CHICKEN THIGHS WITH LEMON COUSCOUS

SERVES: 4 | **PREP:** 15 MINUTES | **STAND/CHILL:** 10–15 MINUTES | **COOK:** 12–15 MINUTES

2 tbsp rose harissa paste

2 tbsp clear honey

finely grated zest and juice
of 1 lemon

pinch of sumac (optional)

1 tbsp olive oil, plus extra
for brushing

12 chicken thighs, bone in,
skin on

Lemon couscous:

400g/14oz (2¼ cups)
couscous (dry weight)

60ml/2fl oz (¼ cup) olive oil

juice of 1 lemon

480ml/16fl oz (2 cups)
boiling chicken stock

50g/2oz (½ cup) pine nuts

skin of 3 preserved lemons,
diced (pips and flesh
removed)

85g/3oz (½ cup) sultanas
(seedless raisins)

200g/7oz (¾ cup) canned
chickpeas, rinsed and
drained

1 small bunch of spring
onions (scallions), chopped

handful of flat-leaf parsley,
chopped

sea salt and freshly ground
black pepper

You can buy rose harissa in most delis and the specialist sections of many supermarkets. It tastes slightly sweet and smoky but is intensely aromatic with the same fiery heat of regular harissa.

1 In a bowl, mix together the rose harissa, honey, lemon zest and juice, sumac (if using) and 1 tablespoon olive oil. Add the chicken thighs and turn them over in the mixture until well coated. Cover and chill in the fridge for 15 minutes while you prepare the couscous.

2 Make the couscous: put the couscous, olive oil and lemon juice in a large heatproof bowl. Pour in the chicken stock, give it a stir and then cover the bowl and set aside for 10–15 minutes. The grains of couscous will swell and absorb all the liquid.

3 Toast the pine nuts in a small dry frying pan (skillet) over a medium heat, tossing them gently for 1–2 minutes until they colour. Remove them from the pan immediately and add to the couscous.

4 Stir in the preserved lemon skin, sultanas, chickpeas, spring onions and parsley. Season to taste with salt and pepper.

5 Lightly brush a baking tray (cookie sheet) with oil and arrange the chicken thighs on top. Cook under a preheated hot grill (broiler) for 12–15 minutes, turning occasionally, until thoroughly cooked, sticky and golden brown. Baste from time to time with the leftover harissa.

6 Serve the sticky chicken thighs immediately with the warm couscous.

OR YOU CAN TRY THIS...

– Add some chopped coriander (cilantro) or mint to the couscous.

– Stir in some diced chilli and tomatoes.

– Use regular harissa or green harissa paste instead of rose harissa.

PIRI PIRI CHICKEN WITH SWEET POTATO WEDGES

SERVES: 4 | **PREP:** 20 MINUTES | **MARINATE:** AT LEAST 2 HOURS | **COOK:** 25–35 MINUTES

4 chicken legs, on the bone
600g/1lb 5oz sweet potatoes
3 tbsp olive oil, plus extra
    for brushing
1 tbsp paprika
1 tsp cayenne
1 tsp garlic powder
sea salt and freshly ground
    black pepper

Piri piri marinade:
3 sprigs of thyme, leaves
    picked
3 red chillies, deseeded
    and chopped
3 garlic cloves, peeled
1 tsp paprika
2 tbsp red wine vinegar
2 tbsp olive oil
zest and juice of 1 lemon

This classic Portuguese dish has become very popular in recent years, and deservedly so. You can buy bottles of piri piri sauce and marinade in most supermarkets but it's more satisfying to make yourself.

1 Preheat the oven to 200°C, 400°F, gas mark 6.

2 Make the piri piri marinade: pound the thyme leaves, chillies, garlic and paprika to a paste in a pestle and mortar. Stir in the vinegar, olive oil and lemon juice.

3 Put the chicken legs in a bowl and pour over the marinade. Turn the chicken in the mixture and then cover and marinate in the fridge for at least 2 hours, preferably overnight.

4 Make the coleslaw: mix together the cabbage, carrots, spring onions, apple, walnuts and parsley. Gently stir in the mayonnaise and lemon juice and season to taste with salt and pepper.

5 Scrub the sweet potatoes (don't peel them) and cut into wedges. Put them on a baking tray (cookie sheet) and drizzle with the 3 tablespoons oil. Sprinkle with the paprika, cayenne, garlic powder and some salt and black pepper. Bake in the preheated oven for 25–35 minutes until crisp and golden brown.

6 When you're ready to cook the chicken, lightly brush a griddle (grill) pan or non-stick frying pan (skillet) with the remaining oil. Remove the chicken from the marinade and cook over a medium-high heat for 15–20 minutes, turning occasionally, until golden brown and cooked right through. Baste with any leftover marinade from time to time. The chicken is cooked when it's pierced with a skewer and the juices run clear.

7 Serve the chicken immediately with the hot sweet potato wedges and the coleslaw.

Coleslaw:
200g/7oz white (or mixed
    red and white) cabbage,
    thinly shredded
2 large carrots, grated
1 small bunch of spring
    onions (scallions), chopped
1 red apple, cored and diced
30g/1oz (¼ cup) chopped
    walnuts
handful of parsley, chopped
120g/4oz (½ cup) light
    mayonnaise
juice of ½ small lemon

**OR YOU CAN
TRY THIS...**

– If you're in a hurry just marinate the chicken in some shop-bought piri piri sauce for 30 minutes before cooking.
– If you really are a glutton for hot food, drizzle the cooked chicken with some hot sauce.
– Chicken wings and even breasts work well marinated in this way. If you're feeding a crowd, buy a whole large chicken and cut into 8 pieces (on the bone) and make double the quantity of marinade.

CHINESE CHICKEN DUMPLINGS WITH SWEET CHILLI SAUCE

SERVES: 4 | **PREP:** 25 MINUTES | **CHILL:** AT LEAST 30 MINUTES | **COOK:** 20 MINUTES

500g/1lb 2oz skinned chicken breast fillets, cut into pieces

2.5cm/1in piece fresh root ginger, peeled and chopped

2 red chillies, deseeded and chopped

4 garlic cloves, peeled

1 bunch of spring onions (scallions), chopped

1 small bunch of coriander (cilantro), chopped

225g/8oz (1 cup) basmati rice (dry weight)

1 tbsp sunflower (corn) or groundnut (peanut) oil

400g/14oz pak choi (bok choy), coarsely shredded

shake of soy sauce

sea salt and freshly ground black pepper

sweet chilli sauce, to serve

Little chicken dumplings are much easier to make than you think. You can prepare them in advance and leave them to chill in the fridge for several hours before cooking.

1 Blitz the chicken, ginger, chillies, 2 garlic cloves, spring onions and coriander in a food processor or food chopper for a few seconds. Don't overdo it. You want to end up with a coarse mixture, not a smooth paste. Season with salt and pepper.

2 Divide the mixture into 20 pieces and shape each one into a ball, using your hands. Place them on a tray and cover with some kitchen foil or cling film (plastic wrap). Chill in the fridge for 30 minutes to form them up. You can leave them longer – overnight – if wished.

3 To cook the dumplings, place them in the top of a steamer or on a heatproof plate covered with kitchen foil set over a pan of simmering water. Steam for 20 minutes or until the chicken is cooked through.

4 While the chicken is steaming, cook the rice according to the instructions on the packet.

5 Heat the oil in a wok or deep frying pan (skillet) set over a medium-high heat. Thinly slice the remaining garlic cloves and add to the hot wok with the pak choi. Stir-fry briskly for about 3 minutes and add a little soy sauce. Stir-fry for 30 seconds.

6 Serve the chicken dumplings with the rice and pak choi, drizzled with the sweet chilli sauce.

OR YOU CAN TRY THIS...

– Add a few drops of soy sauce or nam pla (Thai fish sauce) to the chicken dumpling mixture.

– You can use any hot sauce, e.g. Sriracha or spicy Szechuan sauce.

CHICKEN JAMBALAYA WITH TABASCO

SERVES: 4 | **PREP:** 10 MINUTES | **COOK:** 1 HOUR

2 tbsp sunflower (corn) oil
2 fat spicy sausages, e.g.
    Toulouse or chorizo,
    thickly sliced
4 chicken thighs, skin on,
    bone in
1 onion, finely chopped
2 celery sticks, finely
    chopped
2 green (bell) peppers,
    deseeded and diced
3 garlic cloves, crushed
1 tbsp paprika
1 tsp cayenne
1 tsp crushed black
    peppercorns
2 sprigs of thyme, leaves
    picked
2 bay leaves
600ml/1 pint (2½ cups)
    hot chicken stock
1 tsp Tabasco, plus extra
    for drizzling
350g/12oz (1½ cups) long-
    grain rice (dry weight)
300g/10oz raw king prawns
    (jumbo shrimp)
juice of 1 lemon
4 spring onions (scallions),
    thinly sliced

There are so many versions of this American creole classic dish from the Deep South. Hearty and rib-stickingly filling, jambalaya combines surf and turf and delivers some heat for hot sauce lovers. Tabasco is traditional but you can use most hot sauces, especially West Indian, Mexican and South American ones.

1 Heat the oil in a large deep sauté pan or frying pan (skillet) with a lid. Cook the sausages over a medium-high heat for about 5 minutes until browned, cooked through and the fat starts to run. Remove and drain on kitchen paper (paper towels).

2 Add the chicken to the pan and cook, turning occasionally, for 8–10 minutes until browned all over. Remove and drain on kitchen paper (paper towels).

3 Add the onion, celery, green peppers and garlic to the hot pan and cook, stirring occasionally, for 6–8 minutes until tender. Stir in the paprika, cayenne, black pepper, thyme and bay leaves. Cook for 1 minute.

4 Add the hot stock and Tabasco and return the chicken to the pan. Simmer gently for 10 minutes, then stir in the rice. Cover the pan and cook over a very low heat for about 15 minutes or until the rice is tender. Add the sausage and the prawns and give the rice a stir. Cook gently for 2–3 minutes, then remove the chicken and remove from the heat. Set aside, covered with the lid, for 10 minutes.

5 Remove the cooked chicken from the bone and cut into smaller pieces. Add to the jambalaya and stir in the lemon juice.

6 Serve sprinkled with the spring onions and drizzled with Tabasco.

OR YOU CAN TRY THIS...
– Add some canned tomatoes or chopped fresh ones to the rice.
– Green (bell) peppers are traditional but you could use red or yellow instead for a sweeter flavour.

CRISPY DUCK WITH SZECHUAN HOT PLUM SAUCE

SERVES: 4 | **PREP:** 15 MINUTES | **CHILL:** AT LEAST 2–3 HOURS | **COOK:** 1½ HOURS

4 x 100g/3½oz free-range
    duck legs
1 tsp salt
2 tsp whole Sichuan
    peppercorns, crushed
1 tsp five-spice powder
2.5cm/1in piece fresh root
    ginger, peeled and bashed
    with a rolling pin
1 tbsp Shaoxing wine
    (optional)
180ml/6fl oz (¾ cup)
    chicken stock
16 Chinese pancakes

Chinese crispy duck is easier to make than you think. The hands-on preparation doesn't take long but it's best to start the day before so you can salt and spice the duck legs and leave them to absorb the flavours overnight. You can make the pancakes yourself if you like but it's easier to buy a pack of ready-made ones. They're available in most large supermarkets as well as Chinese food stores and online.

1 Prick the skin on the duck legs all over with a sharp knife. Mix together the salt, peppercorns, five-spice powder, ginger and Shaoxing wine (if using). Rub this all over the duck legs, then cover and chill in the fridge for at least 2–3 hours or, preferably, overnight.

2 Preheat the oven to 200°C, 400°F, gas mark 6.

3 Gently press some kitchen paper (paper towels) on to the duck legs to dry them and put them in a large frying pan (skillet) over a medium-high heat. When the skin is really golden brown and crisp underneath, turn them over and brown the other side. Drain off the fat as you go along.

4 Put the duck legs in a baking dish and pour the stock around them. Cook in the preheated oven for 25 minutes, then reduce the heat to 140°C, 275°F, gas mark 1 and leave for 1 hour. The skin should be really crisp and the meat falling off the bones. Using two forks, remove the meat and skin from the bones and shred it.

To serve:
½ cucumber, cut into thin
matchsticks
1 bunch of spring onions
(scallions), white parts
only, shredded
Szechuan hot plum sauce
(see page 20)

5 Meanwhile, warm the pancakes in some baking parchment (parchment paper) or kitchen foil in a steamer set over a pan of simmering water. Alternatively, warm them in a microwave.

6 To serve, arrange the duck on a large serving platter with the cucumber matchsticks and spring onions on the side. Fill some small individual dishes or ramekins with the Szechuan hot plum sauce. Keep the pancakes warm in a bamboo steamer basket or cover with a cloth. Guests can help themselves to pancakes, spread them with the hot plum sauce, sprinkle with a little cucumber and spring onion, then top with duck and fold over or roll up the pancakes.

OR YOU CAN TRY THIS...

– Add a crushed cinnamon stick and a star anise to the marinade mixture.
– Instead of hot plum sauce, use bottled hoisin and stir in a little Tabasco to give it some heat.

BRAZILIAN COCONUT PRAWN (SHRIMP) STEW

SERVES: 4 | **PREP:** 15 MINUTES | **MARINATE:** 10–15 MINUTES | **COOK:** 20 MINUTES

600g/1lb 5oz peeled raw large prawns (jumbo shrimp), deveined
juice of 2 limes
2 tbsp olive oil
1 large onion, diced
3 garlic cloves, crushed
1 red (bell) pepper, deseeded and chopped
1 green (bell) pepper, deseeded and chopped
1 red chilli, deseeded and cut into thin slivers
3 large juicy tomatoes, coarsely chopped
400ml/14fl oz (generous 1½ cups) canned coconut milk
1 bunch of coriander (cilantro), finely chopped
225g/8oz (1 cup) basmati rice (dry weight)
sea salt and freshly ground black pepper
Brazilian hot sauce, for drizzling
lime wedges, to serve

Hot sauce, made with fiery chilli peppers, is a staple in Brazilian kitchens. It's similar to the Portuguese piri piri (*pimenta caseira*), so you can use this if you can't find the real thing.

1 Put the prawns and lime juice in a bowl and leave in a cool place to marinate for about 10–15 minutes while you start cooking.

2 Heat the oil in a large frying pan (skillet) set over a medium heat. Cook the onion, garlic, peppers and chilli, stirring occasionally, for 6–8 minutes, until tender.

3 Stir in the tomatoes and cook for 1 minute. Season with salt and pepper, then add the coconut milk and half the coriander. Reduce the heat and simmer for 5 minutes.

4 Add the prawns in the lime juice marinade and continue cooking for about 5 minutes until the prawns turn pink and the sauce reduces a little. Stir in the remaining coriander.

5 Meanwhile, cook the rice according to the packet instructions.

6 Divide the rice between 4 shallow bowls and ladle the coconut prawn stew over the top. Drizzle with hot sauce and serve immediately with lime wedges.

OR YOU CAN TRY THIS...
– For a really hot version, add a few drops of hot sauce or Tabasco to the stew.
– Use a red onion and sprinkle shredded spring onions (scallions) over the finished dish.
– For an authentic flavour and look, use palm oil instead of olive oil (*dendê* in Brazil).
– Substitute a can of chopped tomatoes for fresh, chopped ones.

GRIDDLED STEAKS WITH GREEN TABASCO BUTTER

SERVES: 4 | **PREP:** 15 MINUTES | **COOK:** 45–50 MINUTES

2 tbsp olive oil
4 corn cobs, husks removed
4 lean sirloin or rump steaks
sea salt and freshly ground
    black pepper

Green Tabasco butter:
1 garlic clove, crushed
few sprigs of parsley, finely
    chopped
4 spring onions (scallions),
    thinly sliced
125g/4oz (1 stick) butter,
    softened (at room
    temperature)
few drops of green Tabasco

Avocado salsa:
1 ripe avocado, peeled,
    stoned (pitted) and diced
225g/8oz cherry tomatoes,
    quartered
½ red onion, diced
handful of coriander
    (cilantro), chopped
juice of 1 lime
green Tabasco, to taste
sea salt, to taste

A really simple meal that you can throw together without any fuss. You can make the Tabasco butter in advance and keep a roll in the freezer for topping grilled meat, fish and vegetables. Green Tabasco is sold in most supermarkets and is milder than the more familiar red sauce.

1 Preheat the oven to 190°C, 375°F, gas mark 5.

2 Brush 1 tablespoon olive oil over the corn cobs and place on a baking tray (cookie sheet). Season with salt and pepper. Bake in the preheated oven for 35–40 minutes until the corn kernels are tender.

3 Meanwhile, make the green Tabasco butter: grind the garlic, parsley, spring onions and a pinch of salt in a pestle and mortar to a green paste. Blend with the softened butter and add a few drops of Tabasco. Place the flavoured butter on some cling film (plastic wrap) and roll into a sausage shape, twisting the ends. Chill in the fridge or freezer.

4 Make the avocado salsa: mix all the ingredients together in a bowl, adding Tabasco and salt to taste. Set aside in the fridge or a cool place.

5 Brush the steaks with the remaining oil and season with salt and pepper. When you're ready to cook it, heat a ridged griddle (grill) pan over a high heat and when it's really hot, add the steaks. Cook for 2–3 minutes each side depending on how well cooked you like them.

6 Remove the Tabasco butter roll from the fridge or freezer and cut into 4 slices. Put a slice on top of each hot steak and serve immediately with the roasted corn cobs and avocado salsa.

OR YOU CAN TRY THIS...
– Make extra Tabasco butter and dot over the hot corn before serving.
– Dust the corn with cayenne or chilli powder before cooking.

LEMONGRASS PORK SKEWERS WITH HOT SAUCE

SERVES: 4 | **PREP:** 20 MINUTES | **COOK:** 10–15 MINUTES

10 long lemongrass stalks
500g/1lb 2oz (2¼ cups) minced (ground) pork
1 garlic clove, crushed
4 spring onions (scallions), finely chopped
handful of coriander (cilantro), chopped
grated zest of 1 lime
1 tbsp nam pla (Thai fish sauce)
2 tsp cornflour (cornstarch)
1 tbsp Thai hot sauce, e.g. Sriracha, plus extra for drizzling
oil, for brushing
boiled rice or rice noodles, to serve

Stir-fried cabbage:
1 tbsp coconut oil or sunflower (corn) oil
1 tsp black mustard seeds
2.5cm/1in fresh root ginger, peeled and diced
400g/14oz green cabbage, spring greens or kale, coarsely shredded
few drops of soy sauce

These pretty Thai pork skewers are wonderfully spicy and fragrant. You can cook them under an overhead grill (broiler), on a griddle (grill) pan or over glowing hot coals on a barbecue.

1 Peel the lemongrass stalks, removing the outer layers until you get to the smoother inner stalk. Set 8 stalks aside and slice the remaining stalks as thinly as possible.

2 Put the sliced lemongrass in a bowl with the pork mince, garlic, spring onions, coriander and lime zest. Mix well. Blend the nam pla and cornflour and stir into the mixture with the hot sauce.

3 Divide the mixture into 8 evenly sized portions and mould each one round a lemongrass stalk, leaving a little exposed at both ends. Lightly brush with oil.

4 Cook under a preheated hot grill (broiler) placed on a rack above a grill (broiler) pan to catch the fat as it drips out. Turn the skewers occasionally until thoroughly cooked through and golden brown on the outside. This will take about 10 minutes or so.

5 Meanwhile, make the stir-fried cabbage: heat the oil in a wok or deep frying pan (skillet) over a medium heat and cook the mustard seeds and ginger for 1 minute until the seeds pop and release their aroma. Add the cabbage and stir-fry for 2–3 minutes until just tender. Add a shake of soy sauce.

6 Serve the skewers, drizzled with hot sauce, with the stir-fried cabbage and some rice or noodles.

OR YOU CAN TRY THIS...
– Serve the skewers wrapped in crisp lettuce leaves.
– Use wooden skewers soaked in water instead of lemongrass stalks.

SRIRACHA SALMON FILLETS WITH NOODLES

SERVES: 4 | **PREP:** 10 MINUTES | **CHILL:** 30 MINUTES | **COOK:** 15 MINUTES

1 tbsp white miso
1 tbsp Sriracha, plus extra
  for drizzling
1 tsp sesame oil
2 tsp sunflower (corn) oil
2.5cm/1in piece fresh root
  ginger, peeled and grated
pinch of salt
4 salmon fillets, skinned

Noodles:
300g/10oz egg noodles
1 tsp sesame oil
1 bunch of spring onions
  (scallions), sliced
  diagonally
400g/14oz baby spinach
  leaves
100g/3½oz (1 cup) bean
  sprouts
2 tbsp Japanese soy sauce
2 tbsp black or white sesame
  seeds

Oily fish is so healthy and a great source of heart-friendly omega-3 oil that you should try to eat it at least once a week. Salmon lends itself to hot, spicy flavourings and here we've used Sriracha to give it a lift.

1 In a bowl, mix together the miso, Sriracha, sesame and sunflower oils and ginger. Add the salt and stir well. Place the salmon fillets on a sheet of kitchen foil and brush with the Sriracha miso glaze. Turn the salmon over and brush the other side. Wrap them loosely in the foil and set aside in a cool place for 30 minutes.

2 Preheat the oven to 180°C, 350°F, gas mark 4.

3 Remove the salmon fillets from the foil and place in a baking dish. Bake in the preheated oven for 15 minutes or until the fish is cooked right through.

4 Meanwhile, cook the noodles according to the instructions on the packet, then drain.

5 Heat the oil in a wok or deep frying pan (skillet) set over a high heat. Add the spring onions and stir-fry for 2 minutes. Stir in the spinach and bean sprouts and cook for 2 minutes. Add the drained noodles, soy sauce and sesame seeds and stir-fry for 1 minute.

6 Divide the noodles between 4 shallow serving dishes and top each one with a salmon fillet. Spoon over any remaining marinade in the dish.

OR YOU CAN TRY THIS...

– Add some carrot matchsticks and thinly sliced red or yellow (bell) peppers to the stir-fried noodles.
– Use rice noodles or Japanese soba noodles.
– Substitute teriyaki sauce for soy and use pak choi (bok choy) instead of spinach.

CAPONATA WITH TOMATO CHILLI JAM

SERVES: 4 | **PREP:** 15 MINUTES | **COOK:** 50–55 MINUTES

5 tbsp fruity green olive oil

500g/1lb 2oz aubergines (eggplants), cubed

1 large courgette (zucchini), cubed

1 large red onion, thinly sliced

2 garlic cloves, crushed

2 celery sticks, diced

1 red (bell) pepper, deseeded and cut into chunks

200g/7oz juicy tomatoes, diced

1 x 200g/7oz can (1 cup) chopped tomatoes

85ml/3fl oz (⅓ cup) red wine vinegar

30g/1oz (scant ¼ cup) salted capers, rinsed

60g/2oz stoned (pitted) green olives

60g/2oz (½ cup) sultanas (seedless raisins)

2 tsp caster (superfine) sugar

1–2 tbsp tomato chilli jam (see page 22)

45g/1½oz (scant ½ cup) toasted pine nuts

bunch of flat-leaf parsley, chopped

sea salt and freshly ground black pepper

crusty bread or warmed pitta bread, to serve

This Sicilian vegetable stew is so versatile – you can use it as a sauce for pasta, as a topping for couscous, quinoa or freekeh or as part of an antipasto platter.

1 Heat the olive oil in a large deep frying pan (skillet) or a sauté pan with a lid over a medium heat. Add the aubergines and cook, stirring occasionally, for about 5 minutes until tender and golden brown all over. Remove with a slotted spoon and drain on kitchen paper (paper towels).

2 Add the courgette to the pan and cook, stirring occasionally, for 4–5 minutes until golden brown all over. Remove and drain on kitchen paper (paper towels).

3 Add the onion, garlic, celery and red pepper and cook, stirring often, until softened – 6–8 minutes. Stir in the fresh and canned tomatoes and the vinegar and reduce the heat to a simmer. Add the capers, olives, sultanas, sugar and tomato chilli jam and then stir in the cooked aubergines and courgette. Season to taste with salt and pepper.

4 Cover the pan with a lid and simmer gently on the lowest possible heat for at least 30 minutes or until the vegetables are really tender and the liquid has reduced and thickened. Check from time to time and if it's a bit dry, add a little water to moisten it.

5 Meanwhile, in a small dry frying pan (skillet) toast the pine nuts over a medium-high heat for 12 minutes, tossing them gently. When they are golden brown, remove from the pan immediately before they burn.

6 Stir most of the parsley into the caponata and sprinkle the rest over the top with the toasted pine nuts. Serve lukewarm or even cold with crusty bread or warmed pitta bread.

OR YOU CAN TRY THIS...

– If you don't have any tomato chilli jam, add ½ tsp harissa paste instead.
– Add some thinly sliced fennel bulb and some chopped feathery fronds.

VEGGIE NASI GORENG

SERVES: 4 | **PREP:** 15 MINUTES | **CHILL:** 1 HOUR | **COOK:** 35–40 MINUTES

450g/1lb (2 cups) long-grain rice (dry weight)

3 tbsp groundnut (peanut) oil

4 medium free-range eggs, beaten

2 large onions, thinly sliced

4 garlic cloves, crushed

1 red (bell) pepper, deseeded and thinly sliced

2 carrots, diced

1 tsp sambal oelek

250g/9oz broccoli florets

350g/12oz Chinese leaf (Chinese cabbage), shredded

1 small bunch of spring onions (scallions), thinly sliced

handful of coriander (cilantro), chopped

1 red chilli, thinly sliced

60g/2oz (½ cup) roasted peanuts, coarsely chopped

sea salt and freshly ground black pepper

lime wedges, to serve

Indonesian hot sauce:
2 tbsp sweet chilli sauce

2 tbsp kecap manis (Indonesian sweet soy sauce)

Sambal oelek is commonly used throughout Indonesia and Malaysia to flavour a wide range of dishes. It's the distilled essence of what constitutes a hot sauce: ground hot red chillies, vinegar and salt.

1 Cook the rice according to the instructions on the packet. Drain and spread it out on a large baking tray (cookie sheet). Fluff it up with a fork and leave to cool. When it's cold, cover and chill in the fridge for at least 1 hour.

2 Make the Indonesian hot sauce: mix together the sweet chilli sauce and kecap manis in a small jug or bowl.

3 When you're ready to start cooking, heat a little oil in a large non-stick frying pan (skillet) over a medium heat. Pour in the beaten eggs and some salt and pepper, tilting the pan to spread it evenly. Stir with a fork and, as it starts to set, gently lift the edges so any liquid can flow underneath. When the underside is set and golden, slide the omelette out of the pan. Roll up and cut into thin slices.

4 Heat the remaining oil in a wok or deep frying pan (skillet) set over a medium to high heat. Add the onions, garlic, red pepper and carrots. Stir-fry for 3–4 minutes. Stir in the sambal oelek, broccoli and Chinese leaf and stir-fry for 2–3 minutes.

5 Tip in the rice and the Indonesian hot sauce and heat through, stirring often to prevent the rice sticking and to distribute the heat, for about 5 minutes until everything is piping hot. Stir in the spring onions and coriander and check the seasoning.

6 Divide between 4 shallow serving dishes and top with the omelette strips, chilli and peanuts. Serve immediately with lime wedges.

OR YOU CAN TRY THIS...

– Add some cubes of tofu, thin green beans or bean sprouts.

– Instead of omelette strips, top each portion with a fried egg.

DESSERTS, BAKING & DRINKS

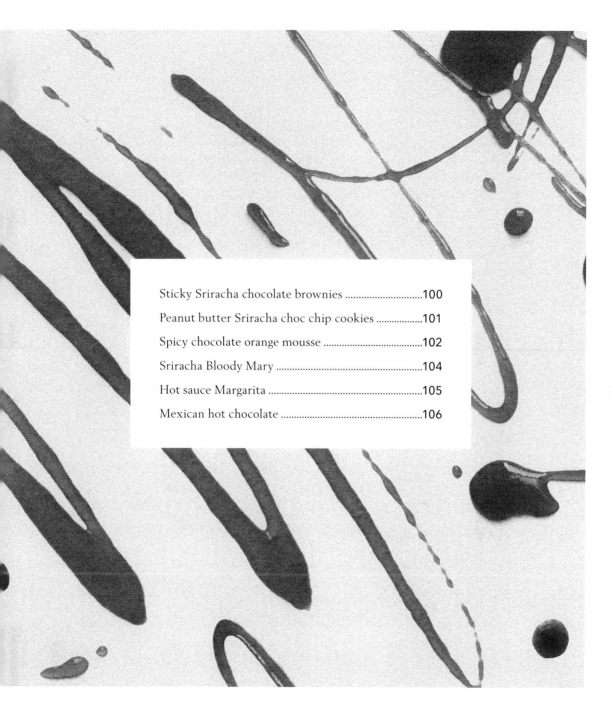

STICKY SRIRACHA CHOCOLATE BROWNIES

MAKES: 12 SQUARES | **PREP:** 15 MINUTES | **COOK:** 25–30 MINUTES

250g/9oz (2 sticks) butter (at room temperature), plus extra for greasing
300g/10oz (1½ cups) caster (superfine) sugar
4 medium free-range eggs, beaten
225g/8oz dark (bittersweet) chocolate (70% cocoa solids), broken into squares
1 tbsp Sriracha
60g/2oz (½ cup) plain (all-purpose) flour
60g/2oz (½ cup) cocoa powder
½ tsp baking powder
125g/4oz (scant ¾ cup) chopped hazelnuts

Chilli powder is sometimes added to brownies but Sriracha tastes even better and gives these sticky chocolate squares a real kick. Serve them as a snack or teatime treat, or even as a dessert with ice cream or crème fraîche and berries – raspberries, strawberries, redcurrants or cherries.

1 Preheat the oven to 180°C, 350°F, gas mark 4. Lightly grease a 23cm/9in cake tin (baking pan) with butter and line with baking parchment (parchment paper).

2 Beat the butter and sugar in a food mixer (or with an electric hand-held whisk) until soft, creamy and fluffy. Whisk in the beaten eggs, a little at a time.

3 Meanwhile, put three-quarters of the chocolate in a heatproof bowl suspended over a pan of simmering water. When it has melted, remove from the heat.

4 Stir the melted chocolate into the cake mix with a metal spoon. Chop the remaining chocolate into little chunks and add to the mixture with the Sriracha. Sift in the flour, cocoa and baking powder and fold in gently in a figure-of-eight movement. Lastly, stir in the nuts.

5 Pour the mixture into the prepared tin and level the top. Bake in the preheated oven for 25–30 minutes or until risen and a skewer inserted into the centre comes out slightly gooey but not raw.

6 Leave to cool in the tin before cutting the brownies into squares.

OR YOU CAN TRY THIS...
– Instead of hazelnuts use chopped walnuts or pecans.
– Use 2 teaspoons Tabasco instead of Sriracha.
– You can add a few drops of vanilla extract or some grated orange zest.

PEANUT BUTTER SRIRACHA CHOC CHIP COOKIES

MAKES: 12 | **PREP:** 15 MINUTES | **COOK:** 10–12 MINUTES

200g/7oz (scant 1 cup)
   crunchy peanut butter
125g/4oz (generous ½ cup)
   caster (superfine) sugar
60g/2oz (generous ¼ cup)
   soft brown sugar
1 tbsp plain (all-purpose)
   flour
pinch of sea salt crystals,
   plus extra for sprinkling
1 medium free-range egg,
   beaten
2 tsp Sriracha
4 tbsp dark (bittersweet)
   chocolate chips

These cookies are really quick and easy to make using store cupboard ingredients. If you have a sweet tooth, you can sprinkle them with a little sugar instead of salt just before baking.

1 Preheat the oven to 180°C, 350°F, gas mark 4. Line 2 baking trays (cookie sheets) with baking parchment (parchment paper).

2 Mix the peanut butter, sugars, flour, salt, beaten egg and Sriracha together in a bowl. Stir in the chocolate chips and mix to a stiff dough.

3 Divide the dough into 12 pieces and shape each one into a ball. Place them on the lined baking trays, spacing them out well with plenty of room around them. Press down lightly on each ball with a fork to flatten it out and sprinkle lightly with a few sea salt flakes.

4 Bake in the preheated oven for 10–12 minutes until golden brown. Leave to cool for 10 minutes before transferring the cookies to a wire rack. Store the cookies in an airtight container for up to 5 days.

OR YOU CAN TRY THIS...
– Use white or milk chocolate chips.
– Add some vanilla extract or ground cinnamon.
– Add some chopped cashews, walnuts or hazelnuts.
– Use 1 tsp Tabasco instead of Sriracha.
– Use cashew nut butter instead of peanut butter.

SPICY CHOCOLATE ORANGE MOUSSE

SERVES: 4 | **PREP:** 15 MINUTES | **COOK:** 5 MINUTES | **CHILL:** AT LEAST 2 HOURS

250g/9oz dark (bittersweet) chocolate (70% cocoa solids), broken into squares

30g/1oz butter

1 tbsp hot sauce, e.g. Sriracha or Tabasco

2 tbsp hot water

4 medium free-range eggs, separated

½ tsp crushed cardamom seeds

45g/1½oz dark muscovado sugar

grated zest of 1 orange

candied orange peel and shaved dark chocolate, to decorate

This dairy-free chocolate mousse is spiced with cardamom seeds and hot sauce. The muscovado sugar imparts a slight caramel flavour that complements the bitter orange zest and peel. You can make it in advance and chill it until you're ready to serve.

1 Put the chocolate in a heatproof bowl suspended over a pan of simmering water. When it has melted, remove from the heat and gently stir in the butter, hot sauce and water. Alternatively, melt the chocolate in a microwave then add the other ingredients. Set aside to cool for 2–3 minutes.

2 Meanwhile, beat the egg yolks with the cardamom seeds, sugar and orange zest. Stir into the melted chocolate.

3 Whisk the egg whites in a clean dry bowl until they form stiff peaks. Gently fold into the chocolate mixture, a spoonful at a time, using a metal spoon in a figure-of-eight motion. Don't overwork the mixture or you will knock the air out and the mousse will not be light.

4 Divide the mixture between 4 glasses or ramekins and cover with cling film (plastic wrap). Chill in the fridge for at least 2 hours or until set.

5 Decorate the mousses with candied orange peel and chocolate shavings before serving.

OR YOU CAN TRY THIS...
– Use espresso coffee instead of hot water.
– Flavour it with vanilla or finely diced ginger.
– Use white chocolate.

SRIRACHA BLOODY MARY

SERVES: 4 | **PREP:** 5 MINUTES | **CHILL:** AT LEAST 1 HOUR

480ml/16fl oz (2 cups)
     tomato juice
juice of 2 lemons
1 tsp Worcestershire sauce
2 tsp horseradish
pinch of celery salt
1 tsp Sriracha or to taste
freshly ground black pepper
240ml/8fl oz (1 cup) vodka
ice, to serve
4 thin celery stalks or long,
     thin baby carrots with
     feathery tops, to serve

You don't have to be the worse for wear after a big night out to enjoy a Bloody Mary. It's a refreshing cocktail at any time of day, especially in the summer. We've used Sriracha instead of Tabasco in this recipe.

1 Put the tomato and lemon juice, Worcestershire sauce, horseradish and celery salt in a large jug (pitcher). Stir well and add the Sriracha, a little at a time, until you have the right heat. Season with freshly ground black pepper.

2 Cover the jug and chill in the fridge for at least 1 hour or overnight.

3 Stir in the vodka and divide between 4 tall glasses filled with ice. Add a celery stick or carrot to each glass and serve immediately.

OR YOU CAN TRY THIS...

– Garnish with lemon or lime wedges, olives or small cherry tomatoes on cocktail sticks (toothpicks), cornichons or tiny red chillies.
– Use a few drops of Tabasco instead of Sriracha.
– Use lime juice instead of lemon juice.
– Substitute wasabi for horseradish (you may need only 1 teaspoon).
– Add some grated fresh root ginger.
– Sprinkle with snipped chives.

SRIRACHA VIRGIN MARY

For this non-alcoholic version, just make the cocktail as above but omit the vodka. Make sure you use a really good-quality tomato juice or, better still, passata, for the best flavour. Or put all the ingredients in a blender with 4 chopped spring onions (scallions) and blitz until smooth.

HOT SAUCE MARGARITA

SERVES: 1 | **PREP:** 5 MINUTES

60ml/2fl oz silver tequila
30ml/1fl oz Cointreau or
    Triple Sec
200ml/7fl oz margarita mix
juice of 1 lime
dash of Tabasco or Sriracha
salt, for the rim of the glass
ice cubes, to serve
lime wedges, to garnish

Here's a hot and spicy margarita with a kick to excite your taste buds. We've suggested using Tabasco or Sriracha but you can experiment with your favourite hot sauces.

1 Put the tequila, Cointreau, margarita mix and lime juice in a cocktail shaker. Add 1–2 drops of Tabasco or Sriracha (to taste) and shake well.

2 Salt the rims of 2 glasses: briefly dip the rim of each glass into some water to dampen it and then into a saucer of salt.

3 Pour the margarita into the salted glasses, add some ice and garnish with the lime wedges.

OR YOU CAN TRY THIS...
– Add some fresh pineapple or blood orange juice.
– For a savoury margarita, add some puréed red (bell) pepper.
– Brush a little hot sauce onto the rim of each glass before dipping in salt.
– Rub a cut lime wedge round the rim of each glass before adding salt.

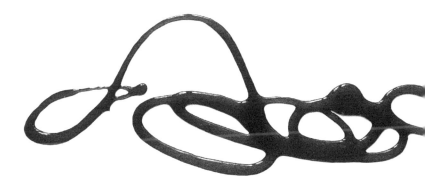

MEXICAN HOT CHOCOLATE

SERVES: 2 | **PREP:** 5 MINUTES | **COOK:** 10 MINUTES

480ml/16fl oz (2 cups) milk
1 cinnamon stick
dash of Mexican hot sauce,
    e.g. habanero pepper sauce
200g/7oz dark (bittersweet)
    chocolate (70% cocoa
    solids), broken into squares
sugar, to sweeten
freshly grated nutmeg or
    ground cinnamon, to serve

In Mexico you can buy special chocolate bars for making this milky hot drink. This hot chocolate is usually spiced with cinnamon or cayenne and whisked for at least 5 minutes in the pan with a special wooden *molinillo* (available online) until really frothy – it's hard work but worth the effort. If you want to try this, you can use a wire (balloon) whisk instead. In Mexico this is traditionally served with *churros*, little deep-fried doughnut-type pastries.

1 Put the milk, cinnamon stick and hot sauce in a saucepan over a low-medium heat. Simmer gently for about 5 minutes until warmed through.

2 Reduce the heat to a bare simmer and add the chocolate. Stir or whisk until it melts.

3 Simmer, stirring occasionally, for about 5 minutes or so until it starts to thicken. Sweeten to taste and remove the cinnamon stick.

4 Pour into 2 mugs and sprinkle with a little nutmeg or cinnamon and enjoy.

OR YOU CAN TRY THIS...
– Use Sriracha instead of Mexican hot sauce.
– Use a few drops of Tabasco.
– Use nut or soya milk instead of regular dairy milk.
– For a much creamier drink substitute double (heavy) cream for one-third of the milk.
– Sweeten with honey or agave syrup instead of sugar.
– Top with whipped cream.

10 9 8 7 6 5 4 3 2 1

Ebury Press, an imprint of Ebury Publishing,
20 Vauxhall Bridge Road,
London SW1V 2SA

Ebury Press is part of the Penguin Random House group of companies
whose addresses can be found at global.penguinrandomhouse.com

Penguin
Random House
UK

Design: Louise Evans
Photography: Joff Lee
Food stylist: Mari Williams
Editor: Lydia Good

First published by Ebury Press in 2018

www.eburypublishing.co.uk

A CIP catalogue record for this book is available from the British Library

ISBN 9781785038389

Origination by Born Group, London
Printed and bound in China by Toppan Leefung

MIX
Paper from
responsible sources
FSC® C018179

Penguin Random House is committed to a sustainable future for our
business, our readers and our planet. This book is made from Forest
Stewardship Council® certified paper.